How to . . .

get the most from your

COLES NOTES

Key Point

Basic concepts in point form.

Close Up

Additional hints, notes, tips or background information.

Watch Out!

Areas where problems frequently occur.

Quick Tip

Concise ideas to help you learn what you need to know.

Remember This!

Essential material for mastery of the topic.

COLES NOTES

How to . . .

Write Effective Business Letters

Correspondence

Memos & faxes

Electronic mail

ABOUT COLES NOTES

COLES NOTES have been an indispensable aid to students on five continents since 1948.

COLES NOTES now offer titles on a wide range of general interest topics as well as traditional academic subject areas and individual literary works. All COLES NOTES are written by experts in their fields and reviewed for accuracy by independent authorities and the Coles Editorial Board.

COLES NOTES provide clear, concise explanations of their subject areas. Proper use of COLES NOTES will result in a broader understanding of the topic being studied. For academic subjects, Coles Notes are an invaluable aid for study, review and exam preparation. For literary works, COLES NOTES provide interesting interpretations and evaluations which supplement the text but are not intended as a substitute for reading the text itself. Use of the NOTES will serve not only to clarify the material being studied, but should enhance the reader's enjoyment of the topic.

COLES PUBLISHING COMPANY
Toronto - Canada
Printed in Canada

Cataloguing in Publication Data
Kelly, Geoffrey M., 1946-
How to - write effective business letters

(Coles notes) ISBN 0-7740-0584-X

1. Commercial correspondence. I. Title. II. Series.

HF5721.K44 1997 808'. 066651 97-932144-1

Editing by Paul Kropp Communications
Book design and layout by Karen Petherick, Markham, Ontario

Manufactured by Webcom Limited
Cover finish: Webcom's Exclusive DURACOAT

Contents

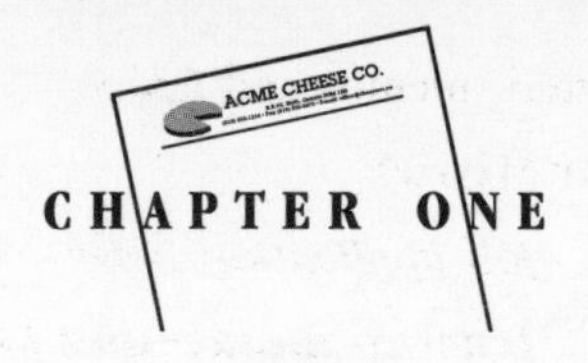

CHAPTER ONE

Word processing & the business letter

Until recently business managers and executives didn't prepare their own letters. They either wrote them out in longhand for submission to a typist or dictated them directly to a secretary or into a Dictaphone. A secretary or typist then typed the letter correcting grammar and spelling, making sure the letter reflected corporate style. Downsizing, desktop computers and word-processing programs have changed this system forever. It is now essential for employees within companies to create quality business correspondence on their own. People who work from a home office should be able to produce letters that look as if they were created in a corporate environment.

Business people at all levels are now creating their own letters, memos and E-mail. This newly found independence is not without its pitfalls. A good secretary is trained in the conventions of business correspondence-skills which include formatting, proofreading, filing and distribution. The quality of the correspondence created by a good secretary reflects this. Unfortunately, many letters created by managers and executives on their own lack this professionalism.

Those who are doing business strictly in Canada and the United States will find the styles discussed in this book will be fine for normal use. Anyone who corresponds internationally should be aware that the expectations of recipients in other countries vary from place to place. The less formal style currently popular in America has already affected Canadian business communication. Overall this trend is good, since it promotes more effective writing. However, the informality acceptable in North America is often not appropriate outside North America. It is best to use the more formal suggestions in this book when writing overseas.

CHAPTER TWO

The difference between personal & business letters

Personal letters - sent from one person to another discussing private matters - might well be handwritten on paper of various sizes, colours, shapes and fragrances. They may be folded in different ways to fit different-size envelopes. The writer of a personal letter usually wishes the correspondence to carry a sense of uniqueness and intimacy; therefore the tone is chatty and the language casual. Because the reader is, presumably, interested in both the writer and the message, the organization of information in the letter need follow no particular pattern. Finally, a personal letter is expected to be read by the addressee only. Its contents ordinarily affect just the writer and the reader. Only in Italian opera do personal letters lead to really important or tragic events; real-life writers rarely worry much about polishing a personal letter or its contents.

Business letters, in comparison, may be addressed to a specific individual, but it is likely that the letter will be read by many people within the company and possibly by parties outside the company. Business letters are written on standard-size paper with a matching envelope, they are typed or printed, and formatted and folded in a conventional way. Most importantly, the content of a business letter is not about personal matters - it conveys an important, necessary exchange of information between people in business. While the effects of a business letter may not be operatically life-threatening, they certainly do influence the course of business, sales, employment, promotion and the company's bottom line. For this reason, business correspondence should be rewritten, polished and proofread before it ever leaves your office.

To further clarify the differences in personal and business correspondence let's compare two examples - one a personal letter, the other a business letter.

Dear Jamie,

Just a word to let you know that the garden is doing fine this year. I just got over a minor operation. Those roses are really looking great. Uncle Harry is doing fine. If he ever gets off the couch, he might even lose a little weight. Maybe when we go to Florida this winter he'll get out on the golf course. Say hi to your Mum and Dad for me.

Love

Auntie Jeannie

P.S. - Let me know if you plan to come visit this summer!

In this letter Auntie Jeannie writes to her niece Jamie to tell her how her garden is doing, that she had a minor operation, and how Uncle Harry is doing. She handwrites it on a half sheet of nicely scented paper and adds a $20 bill in the envelope but doesn't mention this in the letter. A postscript is added as an afterthought. This is a private, charming personal letter between two relatives. No one else will read it. The letter is friendly, pretty, smells nice and contains a surprise $20 bill. Its content will affect no one else, though Jamie will certainly be pleased by the letter and the donation to her personal finances.

February 24, 1999

Mr. Jonathan Smith
President
Ultimate Vending Corporation
7000 Gerard Blvd. West
Montreal, Quebec H3B 1Y9

RE: OVERDUE ACCOUNT

Dear Sir:

We refer you to our letter of February 13, 1999 in which we informed you of your overdue account #345678, and our request for payment. It is now past the 10-day period and we have not received your cheque. We have your next order packed and ready to ship, but until we receive payment this shipment is on hold. Please contact this office by 12:00 noon, February 28, 1999 to explain the arrangements for payment.

Yours truly,

Maria Ricotta

Maria Ricotta (Mrs.)
Credit Manager

MR/ms

cc: Mr. J.T. Gouda - President

The first person to open this letter at Ultimate Vending is the receptionist. The receptionist's duties probably include answering the phone, typing letters, greeting visitors to the office, as well as opening, sorting and distributing the mail. The day the letter from Acme Cheese arrives, there are 50 pieces of mail. This includes 15 pieces of junk mail, five applications for employment, two applications for credit, a request for a reference, a letter from the bank, 10 invoices, 15 sales promos and the letter from Acme Cheese. Each letter must be categorized and sent off to the proper department.

The receptionist opens the Acme Cheese letter. What does she see? It is not junk mail - the receptionist knows this because the letter is printed on company letterhead and is addressed to the president of Ultimate Vending. The words **OVERDUE ACCOUNT** in the subject line immediately jump off the page at her. Rather than allow the letter to wind its regular slow path to the company president, the receptionist takes it immediately to the president's assistant. The assistant reads the letter and understands how important it is for the president to receive it quickly. The assistant will go to the files and retrieve a copy of the March 15 letter and take the whole file into the president for a decision. The letter then might be copied to the credit department or sent over to Ultimate's legal counsel.

The letter is important to both Acme Cheese and Ultimate Vending if the relationship between the two businesses is to continue. Acme wants to get paid. Ultimate Vending may need the shipment to continue operating. The purpose of this letter is to raise a flag, get some attention and keep the relationship going. Acme has already written regarding the account, therefore the tone is cool, abrupt and to the point. Acme's position is expressed in plain, easy-to-understand language. This is effective business correspondence. It affects companies and ultimately the people who work for those companies.

Let's say that the credit manager at Acme did not include the subject line **OVERDUE ACCOUNT** and addressed the letter to the accounting department at Ultimate instead of to the president, or did not advise Ultimate that their shipment was being held. The letter might have become just another reminder of overdue payment and made its way later in the day to the accounting department. There it might have sat in a pile or, worse, ended up stacked in the in-basket of an employee on vacation. The staff at Acme would be angry and hold up their next shipment. The president of Ultimate Vending would not have the opportunity to scramble and come up with a solution until damage had been done. Ultimate Vending would lose a supplier, might lose cheese-loving customers, and both profit and jobs could be lost in the process.

Three Things a Business Letter Should Do

- Convey its message clearly and concisely.
- Give a professional image of the writer and the company he or she represents.
- Produce the response from its reader that the writer intends.

Businesses do not operate in a vacuum. They need to communicate with customers, suppliers, colleagues, government agencies, consultants, employees, politicians and others. The business world is a busy, competitive place and writers of business letters must take care that their letters receive the kind of attention they deserve. Large corporations receive massive amounts of correspondence every day; even small businesses receive considerable amounts of mail. How this correspondence is treated often depends on how professional it looks.

CHAPTER THREE

How to give your letters a professional look

PAPER

Large corporations have custom-printed stationery. A great deal of time and effort goes into the selection of the paper, a logo, as well as the design and placement of the letterhead information. Along with the design elements, the quality of the paper reflects the quality of the company and conveys the importance of the message. Small businesses or home offices can achieve the same result - and save the expense of custom-printed stationery - by configuring a word-processing program to print out a letterhead automatically each time a letter is started.

Letter-size (8 1/2 x 11 in. or 21.5 x 28 cm.) plain white bond is the most common paper for everyday business use. If cost is a factor, utility paper of 20-lb. weight can be used for letter writing as well as photocopying. A small stock of high-quality paper and matching envelopes will suffice for special purpose letters. The paper for these special purpose letters could be a buff-coloured linen in a 24 to 26-lb. weight. The packages of paper at office supply stores contain 500 pages; this is called a ream of paper. You may notice a number on these packages that refers to a weight such as 20 lb. or 75 g/m^2. This is the paper industry's way of indicating the thickness of the paper. Photocopying paper is usually 20 lb. weight and a good linen paper may be 24 lb.

The feel of the paper reflects its weight - thicker, textured paper is usually heavier and more expensive. Business paper, incidentally, should be odorless. Save the lavender-scented stationery for letters to your Auntie Jeannie.

ENVELOPES

The normal letter size for an envelope is #10. This size accommodates up to five sheets of letter-size paper - the number that can be sent with a single stamp. The colour, texture and weight of the envelopes should always match the paper. The normal fold for an 8 1/2 by 11 in. sheet is in thirds - bottom up, top over. If the number of pages or enclosures makes normal folding difficult, it is better to use a larger size of envelope that will accommodate the stack of sheets without folding. If your printer does not allow the direct printing of addresses on envelopes, there are label programs that will print adhesive labels. If you are corresponding with the same company often, you can preprint a whole sheet of labels with the same address.

LETTERHEAD

The letterhead includes the name, address and phone number of the company sending the letter. Most companies have custom-printed letterhead which includes a logo. If your small company or home business does not have custom-designed letterhead, you can create your own with a word processor. An interesting, well-designed letterhead speaks volumes about the company using it. If a letterhead is not available, a simple heading including the company name and address should be inserted before the date line.

CHAPTER FOUR

Formatting business letters

MARGINS

Margins should be a minimum of 1 in. (2.5 cm) for the top, left, right and bottom. If you need a small amount of extra space in order to keep the letter on one page, you may reduce the right margin slightly. A word processor will often preformat the margins, although they may be adjusted using the "page setup" or "format" controls. A well-balanced letter is centred on the page from top to bottom. Once again word processors will do this automatically. If not, make sure there is an equal amount of white space from the bottom of the letterhead section to the date line, and an equal amount of white space from the last line of the letter to the bottom of the page.

SPACING

Business letters are single spaced. Some lines are skipped, however, between various parts of a letter.

FONTS AND FONT SIZES

A standard serif font in a 10 or 12-point size is standard for business correspondence. See Chapter 13 for a more substantial discussion of this and other design issues.

FORMAT

The format of a letter refers to how parts of the letter line up on the page and where certain parts of a letter are placed. These standard letter formats go back to the days when letters were still done on typewriters, and are mostly unchanged today.

The most common letter format is called **full block** in which all the lines are flush with the left margin of the page. This style can be used for any level of formality. **Modified block** has the date and closing lines centered. **Semi-block** is similar to modified block, the most noticeable difference being that the first line of each paragraph is indented. **Simplified block** is similar to full block, but there is no salutation. Punctuation varies from one style to the next. There are examples of these different formats in the section of sample letters. Any of these formats are appropriate for business correspondence.

The "look" of your letter is always the first part of your message.

CHAPTER FIVE

Parts of a business letter

Just as there are parts to the body or parts in a machine, so there are parts of a business letter. Not all the parts are required in every letter, and many can be omitted from memos and faxes. In our discussion, we'll handle some of the fine points of business correspondence.

DATE

The date is inserted two spaces below the letterhead or last line of the address of the sender. The date is placed across the page according to the style of the letter. In full block letters it is flush with the left margin. In modified or semi-block styles it may be centered or flush right. Date a letter the day it is written or dictated since any reference to time in the letter such as "10 days from now" or "yesterday" is calculated by the writer and reader from the date on the letter. The date also becomes a reference for return correspondence such as "regarding your letter of May 5, 1999." This is especially important when "time is of the essence" or there is legal significance to the letter. The month should be written in words such as "April" rather than numerically. The day is expressed as a number with no ordinal abbreviation such as -d, -st, -nd, or -th. The most common form for the date would be "November 28, 2002," though some companies prefer the British style "28 November 2002." Word processors may be configured to insert the date in the format of your choice each time you open a letter file.

INSIDE ADDRESS

The most complex form for the inside address includes the name of the person who should receive the letter, the person's title, the company, number and street, suite or office number, city, province or state and the postal or zip code. The person's name, title and the suite or office number may not be required in a simpler address.

NAME	Mr. Nigel Smith
TITLE	Credit Manager
COMPANY	General Widgets
STREET ADDRESS, SUITE	10 Wimby Street West, Suite 201
CITY, PROVINCE	Toronto, Ontario
POSTAL CODE	M4X 1H5

- The inside address is single spaced.
- A suite or office number may be inserted after the address or separately, on a line before the street address.
- In the case of limited space on the page, the postal code can follow the province on the same line. On the envelope, Canada Post requires the postal code on the same line as the city and province.
- Include a person's title, if known, such as Harry Jones, P. Eng. or Dr. Peter Forrester.
- You may use the two-letter abbreviation for provinces.
- Only insert the country name if the letter is going outside Canada.

Canada is a bilingual country, so when writing in either official language, it is polite to translate parts of addresses into the appropriate language. It is also acceptable to leave an address untranslated. If you have received correspondence that includes an address in French, use it verbatim. The other option is to call the company and get the correct form of the address. If you wish to translate parts of the address on your own, the following suggestions may be useful: words that indicates a type of thoroughfare, such as Street or Avenue, may be translated into the other language.

However, if a word is considered to be part of the official the name of a road, such as 21st Street, it is not translated. Place names are not translated, but the names of provinces and territories may be: Quebec then becomes Québec. The province is always separated from the city name by a comma.

ATTENTION LINE

The attention line indicates that the letter may be dealt with by anyone in the company but is primarily addressed to a particular person. Although considered stuffy or outdated by some, the attention line is still useful in many business situations. It usually appears only in formal letters. It's a good idea to capitalize and bold the attention line. When an attention line is used in a letter, the inside address format is as follows:

COMPANY NAME	General Widgets
STREET ADDRESS	10 Wimby Street West
CITY, PROVINCE	Toronto, Ontario M4X 1H5

ATTENTION: Mr. Nigel Smith

Dear Sir or Madam:

Since the letter is addressed to the company and may be read by someone other than the person named in the attention line, the salutation does not mention the person's name.

SUBJECT LINE (RE:)

A subject line informs the reader of the general content of the letter and provides a reference for storage and retrieval. Traditionally the subject line has been placed after the salutation in the body of the letter. It is now more common to place the subject line before the salutation, two spaces below the attention line, flush with the left margin. The subject line states the topic of the letter briefly. The Latin word "re" meaning "in the matter of" or "concerning" is commonly used to begin this line and then followed by a colon. Some companies use the word **REFERENCE** with a number. Subject lines are used in formal and semiformal correspondence. As with the attention line, the subject line may be capitalized and bolded for dramatic effect.

SALUTATION

The salutation is the greeting that begins the body of the letter. It is inserted after a skipped line below the inside address, attention line or subject line. The salutation should be flush with the left margin. In formal business letters the salutation is followed by a colon; in less formal business letters a comma may be used.

Use these salutations for formal correspondence:

Dear Sir:	*When you're sure the recipient is a man.*
Dear Madam:	*When you're sure the recipient is a woman.*
Dear Sir or Madam:	*When you're not sure.*
Gentlemen:	*When you're sure it's a group of men.*
Mesdames:	*When you're sure it's a group of women.*

Use these salutations for semiformal business letters:

Dear Ms. Smith:	*Dear Terry Smith,*
Dear Mr. Smith:	*Dear Jerry Smith,*

Use these salutations for informal correspondence:

Dear Peter, *Dear Mary,* *Fred,* *Josie,*

These informal greetings are only to be used if you know the person well, and know that this kind of familiarity will not be offensive.

The salutation *To Whom It May Concern:* is going out of style. The phrase has been used for too many suicide notes and in too many Hollywood movies for it to be effective in business communication.

Tips on Names and Forms of Address

- Make sure you have the person's name spelled correctly. Nothing is more objectionable than to begin a letter by misspelling the recipient's name. Call the company to check if necessary.
- If there is any doubt as to the gender of the recipient, leave out Mr. or Ms. and include the person's first name.
- Miss or Mrs. are not used in business correspondence unless you have received a letter from the intended recipient where the individual uses this term of address.

You may have received some correspondence where a formal salutation such as "Dear Mr. Jones" has been struck out with a pen and the recipient's first name has been handwritten over the salutation. Originally this was an excellent technique for adding a warm, personal touch to an otherwise sterile document. Direct mail companies now use this *ad nauseam* and therefore it has lost its effectiveness. If you use this technique, use it sparingly - especially with the same recipient. Never use it in formal documents.

BODY OF THE LETTER

The body of a letter starts after a skipped line below the salutation. Each paragraph is separated by a skipped line. Whether the first line of each sentence is indented depends on the particular format of letter being used (semi-block has the indent; full block does not).

CLOSING

The closing is a polite way of indicating the end of the body. "Yours truly" is the most common closing and is fine for most letters. Flowery closings such as "I remain your most humble servant," while historically charming, are completely inappropriate for modern business use. The range of current closings goes from the informal such as "Regards" to the formal "Yours very truly."

If a letter starts out formally, the closing should correspond. The following is a list of suggested closings from the informal to the formal:

INFORMAL - Friendly

Best regards,	Warmest regards,	Thank you,
Best wishes,	Regards,	

SEMIFORMAL - Friendly, but still businesslike

Sincerely yours,	Cordially,	Cordially yours,
Kindest regards,	Respectfully,	
Respectfully yours,	Sincerely,	

FORMAL - Not particularly friendly, polite, businesslike

Yours sincerely,	Yours truly,	Yours very truly,

SIGNATURE LINE

The writer signs the letter directly below the closing. There is no set amount of space for the written signature but some secretaries report that the amount of space required by the signature line increases with each jump in the corporate hierarchy. Usually three to four spaces is adequate. Some prime ministers, though, have needed up to 12 blank lines to accommodate their signature.

The signature line appears below the written signature. This includes two single-spaced lines, the writer's name and position. Some large corporations place the name of the company after the person's position to indicate that the weight of the corporation is behind the writer of the letter. The section of the letter that includes the closing line and the signature line appears like this:

Yours truly,

John Smith

John Smith
Corporate Vice-President

If the person named in the signature line is unavailable to sign the letter it is common practice to have another sign it and write the word "for" or the Latin equivalent "per" in front of the typed name.

IDENTIFYING INITIALS

This signifies who dictated or wrote the letter and who typed it. The format is as follows: **GK/ps**. The capitalized initials represent the creator and the small initials the typist. If you wish to advertise that you created and typed your own letter you may indicate it by **GK/gk**. The use of identifying initials can be useful if, at some time in the future, it becomes necessary to speak to the person who typed a letter rather than the person who signed it.

ENCLOSURES (Encl.)

Enclosures are items that are included in the envelope but are not part of the letter. This line is placed after a skipped line below the identifying initials and is usually abbreviated to "Encl." It is important to include this line if you are placing documents in the envelope that are not part of the letter. The reader of the letter sees this and expects to find the material in the envelope. If enclosed documents are missing the recipient can inform the writer of the omission. If there is one enclosure, "Encl." suffices. If there is more than one enclosure, the number should be indicated: "Encl. 3".

CARBON COPIES (cc:)

If copies of the letter are going to be distributed to people other than the recipient, then it is customary to list these people. Carbon copy refers to the outdated use of carbon paper to make copies of typewritten sheets. Its abbreviated form "cc" now means "copy sent to." This line appears after a skipped line below the ENCLOSURE LINE. It is business courtesy to list the names of people receiving the copies in the order of their importance in the organization. Titles may be included after each name.

cc: Mary Howard, Director of Sales
David Morgan, Eastern Region
Joe Smith, Sales Associate

BLIND COPY

This is used when you wish to send a copy to a third party without the recipient or the other copied parties being aware of it. The abbreviated form "bc:" is inserted two spaces below the carbon copy line, followed by the person's name. This line appears only on the copy of the letter going to the blind-copied recipient.

bc: George Gardener

POSTSCRIPTS

Postscripts are never used in business correspondence. They give the impression that the writer did not think out the message in the body of the letter. A good business letter, of course, is polished to perfection before sending.

PAGE NUMBERING

There is something neat and clean about a one-page letter. Try to keep your letters to one page. If you have to go to additional pages make sure that each extra page after the first one is consecutively numbered. Page numbering for letters is ordinarily in the bottom-centre position, sometimes with hyphens "-2-" to make a visual impression.

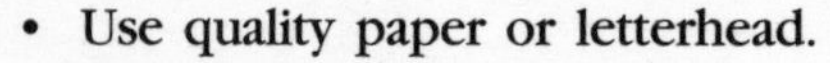

10 Steps to a Good-Looking Letter

- Use quality paper or letterhead.
- Use an envelope that matches the paper.
- Use printed letterhead or create your own.
- Pick a letter format and stick with it.
- Use the appropriate level of formality.
- Always date a letter the day you write it.
- Use a person's title when it is known.
- Use the appropriate salutation and closing.
- Indicate that other documents are included by using "Encl."
- If other people are being sent copies, use "cc:"

5 Things to Avoid

- Never add a postscript to a business letter.
- Never handwrite a business letter.
- Never use scented or novelty paper.
- Never fold a letter more than the normal "thirds" fold.
- Never misspell the recipient's name.

12 Parts of a Letter and Why We Need Them

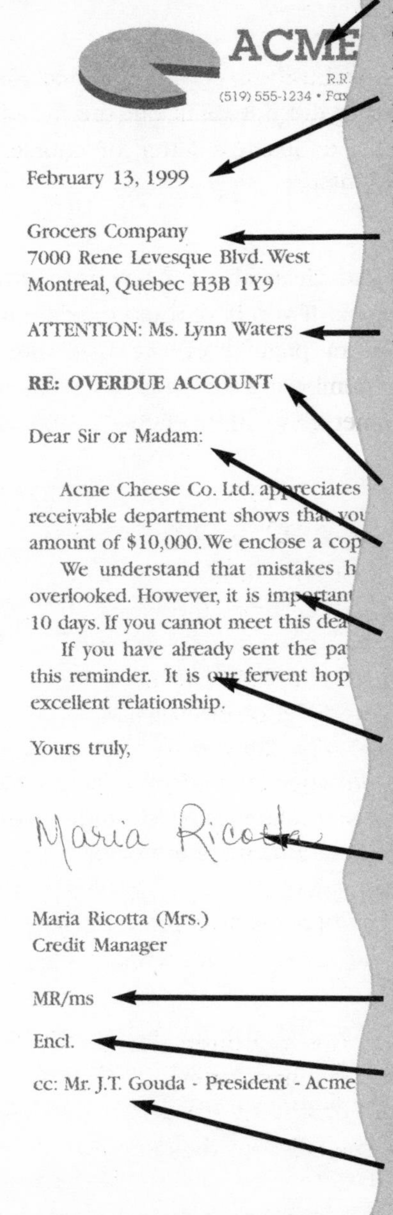

ACME

R.R.

(519) 555-1234 • Fax

February 13, 1999

Grocers Company
7000 Rene Levesque Blvd. West
Montreal, Quebec H3B 1Y9

ATTENTION: Ms. Lynn Waters

RE: OVERDUE ACCOUNT

Dear Sir or Madam:

Acme Cheese Co. Ltd. appreciates
receivable department shows that you
amount of $10,000. We enclose a cop

We understand that mistakes h
overlooked. However, it is important
10 days. If you cannot meet this dea

If you have already sent the pa
this reminder. It is our fervent hop
excellent relationship.

Yours truly,

Maria Ricotta

Maria Ricotta (Mrs.)
Credit Manager

MR/ms

Encl.

cc: Mr. J.T. Gouda - President - Acme

Letterhead: The sending company's logo, name, address, phone and fax.

Date: The date the letter was written; this shows how long it took to arrive and becomes a reference point in any future correspondence.

Inside Address: Identifies the person or department who should ultimately be reading the letter.

Attention Line: Specifies the preferred recipient; but indicates that anyone else in the recipient company might also read the letter.

Subject Line: Prepares the reader for the message in the body.

Salutation: Greets the reader. Can set the tone of the rest of the letter.

Body: Carries the message. An effective business letter is often only one page.

Closing: Signals the end of the message and starts the goodbye sequence. The level of formality is reiterated here.

Signature: Tells who is responsible for the letter and the person's position. Use your full name for most circumstances, your first name with friends.

Initials: Who created the letter and who typed it.

Enclosures: What else should be found in the envelope along with the letter.

Carbon Copies: Who else is receiving a copy of this letter.

CHAPTER SIX

Memos, faxes and electronic mail

HOW TO CREATE AN ORGANIZED MEMO

Memos are a quick, informal way for people within a company, association or group to communicate. By definition, memos are for internal use only. Never use a memo to correspond with other companies.

The hallmark of memos is their brevity. If a memo goes beyond two paragraphs you may want to consider sending the message in a letter. The short, concise message in a memo should be reflected in its layout. Memos are useful when it is necessary to keep a record of instructions or information sent to an individual or group. The posting of memos on bulletin boards is an especially good way to disseminate information to large groups of people.

There is no letterhead on a memo, but some companies have a memo form as part of the company's stationery package. Some writers use the memo templates available with their word processors. Since memos are internal, addresses are not required.

As with other business correspondence, the first line is the date. The **"Date:"** format should be the same as for letters. The month should be written as a word, not a number. A memo is dated the day it is written.

The **"To:"** line is inserted after a skipped line below the date. Since the recipients of memos usually know each other, only the first and second name is necessary without Mr. or Ms. Within large companies it may be advisable to include the department name along with the person's name. For a memo to a group, the word "All" is handy as in "All office personnel" or "All project managers."

MEMO

Date: June 13, 1999

To: Sean Kelly

From: Richard Epstein

Subject: Files for the appeal of the Frost Fencing and Acme Wire case

The files related to the litigation between Frost Fencing and Acme Wire Company are in the Webster St. storage. The appeal to the May 12, 1999 verdict is about to be heard in the Court of Appeals. Please coordinate with my assistants Janet Swanson and Joe Carcone to have the files moved into our office. I'd like this done by June 25.

Distribution:

Janet Swanson
Joe Carcone

The **"From:"** line appears after a skipped line below the "To:" line. Some preprinted memos may include the line "From the Desk of So and So," precluding the need for the "From:" line. Since there is no closing line in a memo, some people initial or sign their name next to the "From:" line, or initial below the body.

There is no salutation.

The **"Subject:"** or **"Re:"** line is more important in a memo than in a letter. Since there is no introductory sentence or paragraph in a memo, the reader's attention needs to be focused quickly. It is, therefore, a good idea to expand on the topic of the memo in the "Subject:" line.

The body appears after a skipped line below the subject line.

The **"Distribution:"** line replaces the "cc:" line used in letters.

ELECTRONIC MAIL (E-MAIL)

E-mail, although it actually describes a means of transmission, has come to describe the documents sent and received this way. Provided that your computer has an E-mail program and a modem connected by phone line to a server, you can transmit your document directly to recipients who are similarly organized. Some E-mail programs are interconnected with word-processing programs and posting is just a matter of clicking a "Send to" icon, filling in the addressee's E-mail address and clicking "Send." This can be further expedited if you have the recipient's name and E-mail address stored in your electronic phone book for automatic retrieval and insertion. Many companies now have internal E-mail systems to cut down on the flow and usage of paper.

ADVANTAGES OF E-MAIL

1. Time and cost savings: no paper, no stamp, no envelope, no trip to the post office.
2. There are no long-distance charges. Your message is sent into a local server and distributed company-wide or worldwide. Transmission outside the company requires a subscription to an Internet service. If you are doing a lot of long-distance correspondence, the cost of the Internet service can be quite economical.
3. The ability to attach documents such as letters or memos that are stored on your hard drive.
4. The ability to send the same transmission to unlimited multiple recipients.
5. The ability to forward a received E-mail to other people - and to respond directly and quickly to the sender.

CAUTIONS ABOUT E-MAIL

1. The process of E-mailing is so fast that there is a much greater chance for you to send rash, ill-thought-out messages or replies. Before you E-mail, make sure you won't regret the contents or tone of your message. E-mail messages can be printed out by the recipient and become part of filed correspondence. With E-mail, you can't run to the mail room and pull the letter out before it's sent, nor can you call the recipient's office a day

later and say "don't bother to open that envelope." Important messages should sit, for as long as you can afford to wait, before you hit the send button.

2. The ease and speed of preparing E-mail can also lead to less time spent on composition. The suggestions on revising and editing letters and memos in other parts of this book also apply to E-mail. A message is a message, however it is sent, and deserves some care in its creation and revision.
3. Be aware that all E-mail programs are not created equal. The different capabilities among systems may result in partial or incomplete reception of your message. For example, the ability to retrieve "attachments" is not universal, and it is standard practice for senders, when transmitting important documents as attachments, to request confirmation that the complete transmission was received.
4. Another disadvantage of E-mail is that some systems have limited graphical abilities and require that documents be transmitted as plain text. This eliminates the effect of any graphical enhancements you may have included in your document.
5. E-mail servers may not deliver your message instantaneously. When a server goes down, your vital message can sit for a day or sometimes be lost forever.
6. The issue of the security of E-mail transmissions at the time of this book's publication has not been resolved. It is always wise to use secure methods of delivery for confidential or sensitive documents.

Business E-mail is still business correspondence.
There is often a tendency to rush E-mail responses, or send them without the editing and polishing you'd ordinarily give to a letter. Be careful. E-mail has an impact just as a letter does. Put yourself in the recipient's shoes before pressing the "send" button.

FACSIMILES (FAXES)

The transmission technology of faxes is similar to sending E-mail except that there is no server between the sender and recipient. Faxes are immediate - faster and cheaper than a courier - and move more quickly than mail in our overworked and underfinanced postal system. However, faxes offer little or no confidentiality in the communication (anyone can read the message as it arrives at the recipient's machine), nor is there any guarantee that your fax will actually make it from the machine to the desk of the person you want to receive it. Still, businesses are increasingly using fax communication for all sorts of ordinary correspondence, so fax routines must be mastered.

ADVANTAGES OF FAXES

1. It is possible to send, receive and store faxes directly by using your computer.
2. Most fax machines print a confirmation page when transmission has been successful. This tells you the fax has been sent and received by the intended machine, but not that it has actually reached your intended recipient.
3. Some fax programs allow for transmission to multiple recipients from an electronic address database.
4. Hard copies of faxes may be filed for future reference or discussion.
5. There are cost and time savings - no envelope, no stamp, no trip to the post office.
6. Unless you have a scanner for your computer, a fax machine is the easiest way to send hard copies of sketches, drawings, photos and handwritten notes over the phone lines.

DISADVANTAGES OF FAXES

1. One major disadvantage of faxes, when compared to E-mail, is that long-distance charges apply. For multi-page documents, these can be substantial.
2. Unless the intended recipient has private access to the receiving fax machine, it is possible that others may read your message. In offices that have a common fax machine, confidentiality of fax information is non-existent.

3. Exactly when a fax will be read is uncertain. Even when your own machine confirms a successful transmission, there is always a chance that the message will not end up where you intended. If the receiving machine is out of paper or ink, the message may be stored in memory or lost altogether.

SENDING AN EFFECTIVE FAX

There are hundreds of years of tradition giving us guidance on the form and protocol of letter-writing, but faxing is relatively new. Stylistically, a fax seems midway between the formality of a letter and the informality of an E-mail. In this way, it most closely follows the form of a memo.

It is now common for companies to have a fax cover page as part of their stationery package. There are also software packages that allow small businesses or home offices to create their own. Most word-processing programs also include a feature for the creation of fax cover sheets and fax memo forms.

The sections of a fax cover sheet are similar to those on memo forms - the main difference is that the word FAX, or some variation, replaces or precedes the word memo. In addition, a fax cover sheet includes a line indicating the total number of pages sent. Since a fax is usually sent between businesses, it includes the sender's name, company name, address, phone and fax numbers, and the intended recipient's name, company and address. Many fax forms have an outlined box for the message.

SOME FINE POINTS ON SENDING A FAX:

- When the information on a fax cover sheet simply duplicates information in the document, it is not necessary to use a cover sheet. Be sure to indicate on the document that the item is being faxed only, or faxed and mailed. The faxed copy is for immediate attention and the mailed copy ensures that the recipient cannot deny the receipt of important documents.
- A standard letter may also be faxed with a cover sheet. The cover sheet confirms who the sender is and how many pages are included. When a faxed document is filed and then later retrieved, the cover sheet will indicate that it was originally faxed.

- The fax cover sheet can become a one-page fax memo form if your message is concise.
- Handwritten documents or sketches, or multiple copies of previously created documents may be sent as a fax. A cover sheet is always needed with these items.

Don't Waste the Toner

The design of some fax cover sheets and promotional material sent via fax may contain a great deal of black area on the page. Large black areas on fax transmissions use up the ink on a recipient's machine. This is inconsiderate and the worst possible way to begin your message. Design a fax cover sheet that emphasizes white space.

Sending massive faxes is also inconsiderate. Faxes of 20 or 30 pages tie up the recipient's machine and also burn out ink cartridges. If you find it necessary to fax a large number of pages, call the recipient to arrange an appropriate time.

Sometimes ordinary mail or a courier will be more appropriate for large amounts of material.

CHAPTER SEVEN

Your message, whatever the medium

Your message, quite simply stated, is the information you want the reader to receive. The first part of your message is always carried by the "look" of your document. When formatted according to the basic conventions, your correspondence tells the reader that the message is from a business, it is professional and the contents have been carefully thought out. While Marshall McLuhan said that the medium is the message, that's not entirely true in business communication. The medium is simply the first part of your message. The content follows.

Experienced writers always consider several factors that influence the message of the letter or memo. These include tone, the person to whom the message is addressed, and how you want the reader to perceive the message itself. It is a good idea, especially if you are not a regular writer of business letters, to consider the following items before beginning to write.

QUESTIONS TO ASK WHEN YOU START TO WRITE

- What kind of person will read the document? Is that person at the upper, middle or lower management level?
- Who else will read my message besides the addressee?
- What flavour do I wish my message to impart?
- What effect do I want it to have?
- What kind of mood am I in? Should I really be writing this letter or memo right now?
- Could this document be used against me at a later date?
- If I am sending a letter, do I need to include "back up" items in the envelope?

WHO IS GOING TO READ YOUR LETTER OR MEMO?

Is the recipient higher, lower or on the same level as you are in the organization? A project manager writing from one company to the president of another company should use a respectful, formal tone; whereas a project manager writing to a counterpart in another company might take a semiformal tone. Business correspondence is usually not completely informal unless the two parties are especially well acquainted and the letter will not be read by a third party.

In an informal letter, the salutation may read "Dear John" rather than "Dear Sir"; likewise the closing can be less formal such as "Kindest regards" or just "Regards." It is always wise to remember that business letters are not private correspondence and may be read by many others even when marked as confidential.

In thinking ahead about your recipient, you should also consider the level of vocabulary and complexity that the reader can comfortably handle. This is usually a function of the reader's level of education. More education usually means a wider vocabulary, although this may not hold true for technical people whose jargon and vocabulary is industry–related. The basic advice of **K.I.S.S.** - keep it simple, stupid - is always a good idea when you are unfamiliar with the recipient.

TONE

The tone of the letter or memo determines how the message is going to sound to your reader. It also gives an impression of the writer to the reader. For example, will the tone sound friendly, formal, curt, persuasive or informative? Will you be perceived as informed, responsible and courteous? This is a major consideration in starting and revising a letter, because the tone of your letter is a big part of its message.

Here is a list that describes various tones of letters:

friendly	*nasty*	*persuasive*	*pleasant*
cold	*warm*	*urgent*	*positive*
apologetic	*conciliatory*	*angry*	*happy*
informative	*respectful*	*annoyed*	*pushy*
opinionated	*unpleasant*	*sarcastic*	*negative*

Which tone would be most appropriate for the message you wish to send? Creating that tone requires you to use care in choosing and polishing your language, deciding how to structure your sentences and listening carefully to the "voice" of your letter.

It is always unbusinesslike to be rude or impolite in a letter. This does not rule out letters that display annoyance and have a definite edge. (See Sample 11 for an example of an "annoyed" tone.) But if you assume a sarcastic tone you will lose the reader immediately. Likewise, a superior or overbearing tone will turn off your reader. Choose your tone carefully - and always let an important letter sit for a day before final revision. Yesterday's anger can turn into tomorrow's embarrassment.

EFFECT

As discussed earlier, business letters and memos are sent for a purpose. Some letters are sent for purely informational reasons. For example, a company might distribute a letter that informs its customers that the office address is changing. No response is required or expected. Another letter, advertising a special price on a certain product, might seem informative but the desired effect is an increase in sales. Another category of letters can be classified as the normal administrative correspondence between individual business people, companies or corporations. These letters are of the back and forth variety. The desired effect is a response or action from the recipient. The method of achieving a "volley" of correspondence depends on both an organized presentation of information and a conclusion that identifies the expected response. See letter Samples 5 and 11 for concluding paragraphs that identify the writer's expectations.

MOOD

We all have swings in emotion. Just as it is good advice to count to ten before speaking in anger, it is wise to pause before writing in anger. Once a letter is mailed, faxed or E-mailed, it is next to impossible to recall it. In the same way, depression caused by personal or business problems can colour the tone of a letter. If you feel unusually down or upset, it's often best to put off letter-writing until your mood improves. How you feel will change in a few hours or days, but what you write in a letter can have an effect that lasts for a very long time.

Careful – letters are legal documents

Letters can sometimes rebound on a writer months after they're sent. For example, a manager of a shipping department writes to a customer and indicates that a certain product will arrive on a specific date without fail. Unfortunately, the product is delayed at the warehouse by an errant employee. The failure to deliver the product on time, as promised in the letter, causes a huge financial loss to the customer. In such a case, the letter might be used in litigation against the shipping manager's company. The point is this - make sure you know the importance of statements you make in correspondence. Money and careers can be lost through a thoughtless sentence.

CHAPTER EIGHT

Organizing your message

It may seem obvious to say that there are three basic parts to the body of a letter - the beginning, middle and end - but like many things in life, the obvious is essential for understanding. A letter without these three essential parts works about as well as a bicycle with one wheel - it is possible to ride such a vehicle, but why put yourself to so much trouble.

THE BEGINNING is either a single sentence or a short paragraph that states the reason you are writing the letter. For example:

We are extremely pleased with the preliminary results of the tests on the A-2000 model, and wish to arrange a further series of tests with you.

The reader immediately knows what the letter is about and should be prepared to continue on with the next section, the details, which can be found in the middle paragraphs.

THE MIDDLE of a letter contains the details. Start a new paragraph after skipping a line below the opening sentence or paragraph.

Unfortunately, the costs for the first series of tests overran our budget. If possible, we would like to reduce the cost of the second series. We are suggesting that both the number and duration of the tests be reduced. As we understand it, there were 20 stability tests and 20 endurance tests. Our feeling is that 10 of each will be adequate for the second series.

The issue of personnel has been raised here and we would like to suggest that Ted Franklin be present from our office. If possible we would like to have Janet McNaughton attend from your end. This arrangement worked well for us last year on the A-1000 tests.

There are two topics in this middle section, therefore there are two paragraphs: the first one discusses costs and the second one discusses personnel. The logical progression is easy to follow, so the reader should have no problem understanding the desires of the writer.

Just as letters have a beginning, middle and end, so do single paragraphs. Although a paragraph may consist of one sentence which could express a complete thought on one issue, it is more usual to have several sentences in a paragraph. This allows for a complete topic to be dealt with. The first sentence of each new paragraph should introduce a new idea; the final sentence should indicate that this topic is finished. What's in between carries all the rest. In school, this is called "hamburger style"; in business letters it's just effective communication.

Large paragraphs - paragraphs with more than four or five sentences - give an unbalanced appearance to a letter, and can become tiresome for your reader. If you find that your paragraphs are lengthy, review them; you may find that you are discussing more than one idea within one paragraph. Then break the paragraph up into smaller ones, remembering that each of those require a beginning, middle and end.

THE END section is a summing up that confirms the expectations of the writer towards the recipient.

There are three things we are going to need before we can issue you a purchase order.

1) *Your response to our idea for the new test format.*
2) *A revised cost quotation for the new format.*
3) *Confirmation of the personnel arrangements.*

If you have any questions about any of this please call us at the main plant. We look forward to hearing from you in the near future.

The end of this particular letter outlines how the reader is expected to act on the information received. The very last sentence is a polite way of concluding the body of the letter. It should also serve as a reminder to the recipient that a response is expected.

Five Simple Suggestions for Letter Organization

- Use a subject line before the salutation and identify the topic of the letter in the first sentence or paragraph.
- Address only one main topic in each letter.
- Use separate paragraphs for each idea or detail within the letter.
- Use lists to highlight points or items within a paragraph. See Sample 1.
- After the topic and details have been taken care of, use a separate paragraph for the conclusion. This should identify your expectations of the reader.

CHAPTER NINE

Getting over writer's block

Sometimes the writers of business letters and memos can experience what novelists call writer's block—the inability to start getting down on paper what you want to say. This may be particularly true if a letter is long and conveys a complicated message. Writer's block is often caused by trying to get the letter absolutely perfect on the first go. Somehow, the right words don't come immediately to mind. And the more you search for those words, the more frustrated you can become.

The solution, as novelists know, is simply to write. Just write something - anything. At least you'll have a few ideas down on paper to edit and revise. The most important thing is to get started. You usually have lots of time, later on, to perfect those initial rough ideas.

If you find this simple wisdom isn't enough, try the following.

1. First of all, if you're really not in the right frame of mind to tackle the particular letter or memo, don't do it! Find something else to do until you are ready. Most business communication will wait a few hours, or even a few days. Meanwhile, your subconscious will be working even when your fingers are not at the keyboard.
2. Once you're ready, sit down and think through the list of questions on page 27. It might even be helpful to scribble an answer to each question.
3. If the stress of the task is still blocking flow of thought to paper, start with one word. Write down a word that describes the topic of the letter. This could be claim, complaint, sales, delivery, accident, whatever the letter is about.

4. Then write out one sentence that explains the reason you are writing the letter. You might be angry about something, or need help on a project, or want advice, or have to break some bad news.
5. The next step is to figure out how many details you will need to explain to the reader in order to cover the main topic of the letter. Do a list of these details without concern for rules or sequence. You can go back over it later to give it a logical sequence.
6. When your list is done, go back and develop a separate paragraph for each detail. Expand these paragraphs, so that all information is covered completely.
7. Write a sentence to describe the response you expect from the reader. Expand this to express completely your expectations on the topic.
8. You'll find that Step 4 gives you your opening sentence, Step 6 gives you your middle paragraphs and Step 7 gives you your concluding paragraph.
9. Now all you have to do is correct the spelling, join or separate sentences, revise paragraphs, polish the style and find someone who will listen carefully to the almost-finished product.

In the past, authors suffering writer's block put off actual writing by sharpening their pencils, or doodling or turning to the bottle. These days, the temptation is to close the word-processing program and open up a game or go cruise the Internet. Procrastination, alas, doesn't get letters written—and it can only add to your problems if someone catches you playing Minesweeper on company time.

CHAPTER TEN

Revising and editing your message

Probably the most useful feature of word-processing programs is the ability to change documents before they are printed. In the pre-computer era, any revision to a typed letter required complete retyping. The result of this time-consuming process was that it was unusual for a letter to be revised more than once. Now, it is not uncommon to revise an important business letter three or four or even ten times if necessary. Thanks to computers we have much greater freedom in editing and revising. This freedom can lead to much better letter, fax and memo writing - but only if you take the time necessary to do thorough editing and revision.

The following are some items to keep in mind when revising your letters and memos:

- Are there any words or phrases that are unnecessary to the meaning? If so, delete them.
- Have you used any long, complicated words that could be replaced with simple words that convey the same meaning?
- Does the letter have a beginning, middle and end?
- Check the flow of ideas in the body of the letter. Does each paragraph cover one detail or idea? Do the details in each paragraph reinforce the main theme of the letter or memo?
- Do the salutation and closing reflect the tone?
- When you read the letter out loud, are there any awkward sentences or phrases that need revising?
- If you notice the same word being used several times, find an alternative. Variety is the spice of life . . . and a key to good letter-writing.

The resulting revisions should produce a document that uses simple, concise language to convey a clear message. It should also embody the tone you intend and produce the effect which you wish to achieve.

One last point about revisions: if there is a particularly good letter-writer in your office - or just a trusted listener - you might want to ask his or her opinion of your efforts. Sometimes what you think you're saying in print isn't what your recipient will be hearing on reading. A little advanced testing can make certain your real message comes across.

PROOFREADING

In pre-downsizing times it was common to have a letter proofread by two people. One person would read the letter out loud and the other would follow the words silently on the page. This technique is rare today, although large corporations and law firms may still do this for important correspondence. Most business people now proofread their own letters by reading them out loud. Any awkward grammar, omission of words, lack of flow or incorrect tone becomes apparent when a letter is read out loud.

The spelling and grammar-checking functions included with word-processor software are often a great help, but be warned that they are not infallible. A spell-checker will not differentiate between words like "too" and "two." Grammar-checkers are great for things like the agreement of nouns and verbs, but they are time consuming since many irrelevant points come up under the category of suggestions. If you have these functions on your computer, use them. Many people who think they are great spellers are surprised at how many errors these programs turn up.

Spelling errors in the final letter leave the impression that the writer didn't respect the recipient enough to take the time to check the spelling. Proofreading or spell-checking will also pick up any typos. Some word-processing programs can be configured to make corrections as you type, but make sure you read what the computer has decided for you. Of course, no computer program can ever catch every error or fix every grammatical problem - that's ultimately up to you.

CHAPTER ELEVEN

Grammar, style and punctuation for business letters

One important concern in business correspondence is to get the simple rules of grammar correct. Failure to do so gives the impression that you, the writer, are unschooled or careless or just plain dumb. For this reason, you should be careful to avoid the most common grammar mistakes.

SUBJECT-VERB AGREEMENT

A singular noun requires a singular verb; a plural noun takes a plural verb. Compound subjects connected by "and" require a plural verb form. This remains true regardless of the number of words and phrases that separate a subject from its verb.

A simple example of a subject and verb not agreeing:

The shipments was delayed.

The shipments were delayed.

Business writers rarely make errors on such simple sentences, but care must be taken on longer ones.

The shipment that we had scheduled to arrive in the last two weeks were delayed by an error at our warehouse.

A longer sentence makes the error less obvious, but it remains an error.

INCOMPLETE SENTENCES

Incomplete sentences occur when either a verb or its subject is missing from the sentence. While this can make for punchy advertising copy, it is rarely suitable for business correspondence.

A solution for cost control, finally, but not for profits.

This sentence doesn't have a verb. A improvement might be:

The department is credited with a solution for cost control, but not for profits.

Incomplete sentences may also occur when a fragment is separated from the main thought.

The shipment is arriving today. Two days late.

Fragmented sentences often occur in a series of short sentences. The fragment is usually an afterthought. One way of correcting the above example might be:

The shipment is arriving today, two days late.

THE RUN-ON SENTENCE

This is the opposite of the incomplete sentence. It occurs when a number of ideas are strung together without pauses. There may be nothing technically wrong with a run-on sentence, but the reader can become confused trying to read a long series of disconnected ideas. The average sentence for business communication should not be longer than 14 words. It is better to break run-on sentences into shorter sentences containing no more than two ideas. The following is an example of a run-on sentence:

There was an accident in the plant, we called an ambulance and Joe wanted to help but the medic had already started first aid.

This series of four complete thoughts can be broken down into two sentences, each containing two ideas. In the first rewrite the sentences have been joined with a comma and the conjunctions *"so"* and *"but."*

There was an accident in the plant, so we called an ambulance. Joe wanted to help, but the medic had already started first aid.

In the second rewrite the sentences have been created by joining two ideas with a semicolon plus a word like "meanwhile."

There was an accident in the plant; therefore we called an ambulance. Joe wanted to help; meanwhile the medic began first aid.

COMMAS CAN IMPROVE YOUR WRITING

The following is a partial list of comma use commonly found in business correspondence:

1. Commas join a series of phrases, words or clauses together. The last item in the series is preceded by a word such as *"and"* or *"or."* Most writers don't use a comma before the conjunction, but this is still a matter of personal preference.

   The office staff increased sales in parts, service and new products.

2. Commas separate two or more adjectives that independently modify a noun.

   It was long, hard work.

   (The test is this: the comma here could be replaced by the word *"and."* If the two modifiers work together, like *well-paid work,* then use a hyphen rather than a comma.)

3. Letters that are made up of sentence after sentence with the same structure become boring and uninteresting. An opening clause or word can draw the reader's attention. This word or clause is separated from the main sentence by a comma.

   Finally, we found the file that you requested.
   After searching the storage space, we found the file that you requested.
   Good news, we found the file that you requested.

4. Sometimes non-essential bits of information in a sentence are set off by commas.

   *The report, **mailed last Friday**, was written by the vice-president.*

5. In parallel constructions it is unnecessary to repeat phrases or words in the second part. They are understood by the reader. The omitted words are replaced by a comma.

   The head office is responsible for salaries; the branch office, personnel.

6. When writing a date that includes the month, day and year, a comma follows the day, e.g. August 12, 1999. When writing a date that includes only the month and the year, a comma is not used: August 1999.

An **EXCLAMATION MARK** gives emphasis to a sentence. If we compare the written word to the spoken word, an exclamation mark is a shout. Since we do not wish to be constantly shouting, exclamation marks should be used sparingly. Any business letter that contains more than one or two exclamation marks should be rewritten or consigned to the trash file of your computer. Similarly, because business letters never *scream*, multiple exclamation marks are not acceptable punctuation.

A **QUESTION MARK** is used at the end of a sentence that asks a question. Sometimes a question mark can be omitted when its use would emphasize the fact that the sentence is a question. This is especially true in long compound sentences.

The **SEMICOLON**, as was discussed in run-on sentences, connects two independent clauses and can be handy for punctuating long items in a list.

Words that can be used with a semicolon to break a long sentence, or join two short ones, include:

likewise	*however*	*otherwise*	*also*
consequently	*as a result*	*nonetheless*	*furthermore*
then	*in fact*	*moreover*	*similarly*
accordingly	*for example*	*besides*	

A **COLON** is used after the salutation (as in *Dear Sir:*) except when the person's first name is used in an informal letter (as in *Dear John,*). A colon is also used when a list is about to be presented in a letter. *There are four concrete samples that we need by tomorrow: the pour at the floor slab, the pour at the retaining wall, the pour at the sump and the pour at the roof slab.*

QUOTATION MARKS are used in business correspondence to set off a quote of someone's direct speech, or when the words or passages are being quoted from another document. *The last time we spoke you said, "The order will arrive on Saturday." It is now Tuesday and...* Quotation marks may also be used to emphasis a word or phrase that is itself the subject of discussion. *Technical terms such as "hard drive," "RAM" and "CPU" are now considered part of the English language.*

End punctuation goes inside quotes.

In the old days of metal type, periods or commas that came after quotation marks frequently broke off in the process of printing. As a result, a printers' convention was established that placed commas and periods *inside* the last quotation mark. *"So," she said, advising the young man, "keep your periods and commas inside to avoid typographical embarrassment."*

ACTIVE OR PASSIVE VOICE

Many writers of business letters unconsciously assume what is called the PASSIVE voice, when the subject is being acted upon, rather than using the ACTIVE voice to show the subject performs the action. Compare the following idea expressed in both passive and active voices.

PASSIVE - *The report was prepared by Janet.*
ACTIVE - *Janet prepared the report.*

The active voice is direct and therefore makes your writing clear and concise. The passive voice is a round-about way of saying something - it can almost seem evasive or apologetic. The words *"was"* or *"were"* are not the only indications of the passive voice, but if they appear frequently in your letters, you may want to check to see if the active voice would be more effective.

This caution does not mean that the passive voice should never be used. It is appropriate to use the passive voice when the person performing the action is unknown or less significant than the action itself.

The contract was signed yesterday.

The Concrete Institute research grant was given to John Doe, P. Eng.

COMMON LANGUAGE ERRORS

One of the major changes in business-letter language has been the move away from outmoded phrases. Compare the following:

OLD-FASHIONED	**NEW-FASHIONED**
Enclosed please find	*We are enclosing*
As per your request	*You requested*
This will acknowledge your recent letter	*Thank you for your letter of June 12*
In lieu of	*Instead of*
We deem it necessary to	*It is necessary to*

If your language sounds stuffy or officious, it probably is. Any idea can be expressed clearly and concisely in modern language.

Repetition

Avoid using the same word over and over. The repetitious use of words becomes boring to the reader. Use a thesaurus or your computer thesaurus to keep the same meaning with different words.

Clichés

A cliché is a phrase that is overused and unoriginal. In business correspondence, clichés lower the level of expression. Probably the only thing worse than a letter dotted with clichés is when the images of two or more clichés conflict. *Our public image, which was once like a breath of fresh air, is now caught between a rock and a hard place.* (Ugh!)

Obscenity, Vulgarity and Slang

Obscenity has no place in business letters. Vulgarity reflects on the writer's character, slang is often in bad taste. The ultimate result degrades the reader's impression of the writer. The kind of language you might carelessly use with a client at a baseball game, or over lunch, should never make it into print.

Racist or Sexist Language

Racist language is completely out of place anywhere, anytime. It should never appear in business correspondence.

Sexist language reinforces stereotypes on sex roles and should always be avoided. One way is to find alternatives to gender-specific words. Here are a few:

mailman - *mail carrier*
chairman - *chair or chairperson*
mankind - *humanity*
policeman - *police officer*
stewardess - *flight attendant*
workman - *worker*
weatherman - *meteorologist or forecaster*

For hundreds of years, writers used the word "he" when the gender of a person in a sentence was not known. The pronoun often used now is *he/she*, though many writers find this awkward. Reconstructing the sentence into the plural form - so *they* can be used - makes for more graceful writing.

When an employee gets hired, he should receive the operations manual.

When an employee gets hired, he/she should receive the operations manual.

When employees get hired, they should receive the operations manual.

JARGON

Industries and businesses develop words and phrases that are specific to their own group. These words are called jargon. Jargon can be a positive factor when individuals are communicating within a group, but be careful not to use jargon when writing to people who may not understand the terms. It can make you sound pompous, or uncommunicative, or both.

SUPERFLUOUS LANGUAGE

Superfluity is the excessive or overabundant use of language. This occurs when writers go overboard trying to express themselves. They may use several words when one is sufficient and correct. When something is pure, for instance, it's pure; it is not 99% pure.

SUPERFLUOUS AND INCORRECT	**CORRECT**
near perfect	*perfect*
approximate estimate	*estimate*
real experience	*experience*
absolutely and totally guaranteed	*guaranteed*

There are many other examples used in common speech. Try not to use them in your business letters.

CONTRACTIONS

A contraction is the combining of two words by shortening and joining with an apostrophe. Contractions are common in daily speech, and therefore can give a conversational tone to an informal letter or memo. See Samples 1 and 14 for the use of contractions to create a warm tone. They should be avoided in formal letters.

The contraction of nouns, such as *Dep't.* for *Department*, is not recommended. Avoid the pitfall of too many contractions in one letter. Test this by reading the letter aloud. Limit the use of contractions to individuals with whom you have developed an ongoing informal correspondence.

Review of Language Usage

- Avoid the use of old-fashioned, stuffy phrases or legalese.
- Avoid repeating the same word too many times in one sentence, paragraph or letter.
- Don't use profanity, slang or vulgarity.
- Use jargon only with people you know for sure will understand it.
- Never use racist or sexist language.
- Watch out for redundancy or superfluity.
- Watch out for words that are spelled similarly but have different meanings.
- Replace clichés with original language.

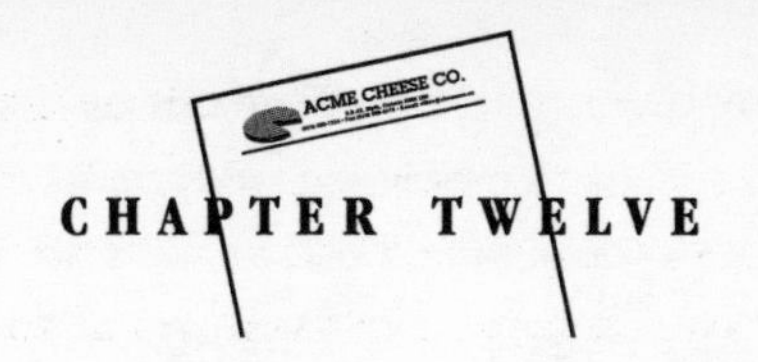

CHAPTER TWELVE

Computers, software and printers

It would be impossible to overstate the benefit of the desktop computer to the business world, particularly to small businesses and home offices. For all but the most special uses, the typewriter is defunct. A desktop computer loaded with a word-processing program and connected to a printer, fax-modem and telephone line allows for easy business communication. Word-processing programs make it much easier to produce top-quality correspondence - no more whiteout, no more carbon paper and sometimes no more paper.

THE COMPUTER

The rate of progress in computer technology is extraordinary. Most desktop systems are outpaced by new systems every 12 months or so. It is therefore useless to suggest a particular specification since it will soon be outmoded. Buy the best system you can afford.

Top-of-the-line computers can handle the newest versions of the popular word processing programs with considerable speed. The potential of these programs goes far beyond the requirements of the average user. If cost is not a factor, you will be able to match a state-of-the-art system with the newest versions of word-processing software. Ultimately these machines are cost-saving devices. They can handle your accounts, database, invoices, faxes, telephone messages, desktop publishing, word processing and a myriad of business-related functions. Most of the new models include a fax-modem, and it is a feature that will quickly pay for itself. If you cannot afford the newest and most powerful computer, there are still many older machines that can be used for basic word processing.

THE PRINTER

There are three types of printers: the dot matrix, ink jet and laser. The reasons for choosing one over another vary from price to the availability of special features like colour printing.

The **DOT MATRIX PRINTER**, although the cheapest to buy, does not print as clearly as the other two kinds of printers unless you purchase the top-end models. The tractor-fed paper common to these printers is unsuitable for business letters, although some models have a sheet-feed attachment.

The **INK JET PRINTER** is moderately priced. It can do either colour or black-and-white printing. Colour printing is rarely used in business correspondence, but can be useful for logos on letterhead or the occasional colour feature on promotional material. A major drawback is that the ink is water soluble and can be easily smudged.

The **LASER PRINTER** is the most expensive to buy, but the quality of print it produces is superior to all other printers. Some of the newest word-processing programs require a laser printer to take full advantage of all their features.

PREFORMATTED LETTERS, MEMOS AND FAXES

"Wizard" functions provide you with a series of choices on how to format a letter, memo or fax. These functions can:

- determine the style of a letter, memo or fax.
- insert the user's name, address and phone number if it is stored in an electronic phonebook.
- insert the letterhead or sender's personal information.
- insert the recipient's name and address salutation.
- add the closing, including the user's name and title.
- insert other parties to be copied.
- insert the enclosure line.

Use of the Wizard procedure can be learned quickly. The time saving is immense.

MULTIPLE "INDIVIDUAL" LETTERS

Once a letter has been created and filed electronically it can be retrieved and used as a basis for correspondence with other recipients. It is important to be careful to edit the date, the "copied to" and enclosure lines for each new letter, as well as to look over the letter itself. While a computer makes it possible to send an "individual" letter to 30 different people by simply changing the person's name and title in the inside address, nothing is more insulting than receiving a "boilerplate" letter that was obviously written for someone else.

Many word-processing programs have a "mail-merge" feature that permits the computer to insert names, addresses and other kinds of specific information into a boilerplate letter. Many hundreds of pseudo-personalized letters can be sent out efficiently by using such a feature. The caution remains – look over the letters before printing them. A computer can't tell that Yonge Street isn't a person's name if you happen to type it in the wrong field column. A few minutes spent eyeballing the letters can save embarrassment later on.

Your spell-checker will not protect you from these common errors:

may be - maybe	*borrow - lend*
accept - except	*altogether - all together*
beside - besides	*conscience - conscious*
adapt - adopt	*all ready - already*

Spell-checkers in word-processing software won't catch misused words, only misspelled ones. Proofread your letter to make certain that it makes sense to you.

CHAPTER THIRTEEN

Designing and formatting your letters

Every word-processing program allows for graphical enhancement of your letters. Earlier versions of word-processing programs basically mimicked the appearance of typewriter fonts. But the most recent software can offer a range of font sizes and styles, symbols such as bullets, and visual aids such as shaded boxes. These enhancements allow for the creation of documents that look professionally printed and effectively get your message across.

In the past, the design of printed material such as stationery was left to professional graphic artists. They knew how to produce visually-appealing designs. Attempts by the untrained to utilize the design features of word-processing programs often produce mixed results. Some people have a natural eye for design; others have difficulty producing good-looking documents. The following is a brief discussion of how to use some of the graphical capabilities of computer software to produce visually-effective letters.

TYPEFACES AND FONTS

New word-processing programs come equipped with dozens of typefaces or fonts – just as a printer in the old days would have a number of different typefaces stacked up in cases beside the ancient printing press. Each font has its own name such as "Courier," " Roman" or "Arial" to differentiate it from other fonts. Sometimes the font name harkens back to the original type designer, or the newspaper where it was first used; sometimes it merely gives a sense of what the type looks like.

The appearance of any individual font may be changed by

bolding, italicizing or small capping. Here are a few samples of fonts and how their appearance can vary.

- Times New Roman
  The rain in Spain falls mainly on the plain.
- Bolded Times New Roman
  The rain in Spain falls mainly on the plain.
- Italicized Times New Roman
  The rain in Spain falls mainly on the plain.
- Bolded and italicized Times New Roman
  The rain in Spain falls mainly on the plain.
- Arial
  The rain in Spain falls mainly on the plain.
- Bolded Arial
  The rain in Spain falls mainly on the plain.
- Italicized Arial
  The rain in Spain falls mainly on the plain.
- Bolded and italicized Arial
  The rain in Spain falls mainly on the plain.
- Courier
  The rain in Spain falls mainly on the plain.
- Bolded Courier
  The rain in Spain falls mainly on the plain.
- Italicized Courier
  The rain in Spain falls mainly on the plain.
- Bolded and italicized Courier –
  The rain in Spain falls mainly on the plain.

Fonts can be divided into three groups: display, serif and sans serif. Serif fonts are the most commonly used typefaces in books and magazines - and usually for letter-writing. The theory is that people are more accustomed to them and therefore more comfortable with them. Serif fonts have those extra bits at the ends of each part of a letter, like the little base under this letter "r." These extra bits help the eye move from one letter to the next. Serif fonts can be used for text, headlines and subheadings.

Sans (without) serif fonts can also be used for body text and display, but they are more difficult to read and therefore they are not recommended for use in business correspondence.

> This is an example of a sans serif font. Some people find it more difficult to read.

The size of fonts for the body of a letter is usually from 10-14 points with 12 point the most commonly used. Fonts of 8 points and below are too small for most people to read comfortably. Headings and subheadings can be a couple of sizes larger than the body text.

Large display fonts should not be used for the text of business correspondence, but are useful when creating letterheads. Some word-processing packages have a feature that will guide you through the creation of a letterhead.

There may be an urge to go wild with type fonts and use many different ones just because they are available on your computer. Try to avoid this temptation by limiting yourself to no more than two typefaces per letter.

Visual variety in the body of a letter can be achieved by the thoughtful use of other enhancing options - bolding, italicizing, underlining and indenting.

Bolding can be an effective way to emphasize individual words or phrases, but only if it is done sparingly.

Compare this sentence with only one word bolded:

> Bolding can be an effective way to **emphasize** individual words or phrases if it is done sparingly.

A similar effect can be achieved by italicizing the typeface:

> *Italic type is another good way to emphasize a word or phrase, if it is used sparingly.*

Once again, compare this sentence with only one word italicized:

> Italic type is another good way to *emphasize* a word or phrase, but only if it is used sparingly.

Overuse of any typographical enhancement makes a letter look cluttered and disorganized. Careful, thoughtful use enhances your message.

BULLETS

The use of lists to help organize details in the middle portion of a letter was discussed in an earlier part of this book. Bullets are square, triangular or round symbols that help to enhance the effectiveness of lists. This enhancement by the use of bullets can be increased by indenting each item. The usual indentation is the standard tab of five spaces.

- The product was defective.
- It arrived late.
- It broke down almost immediately.

The use of bullets for normal office correspondence is linked directly to the graphical ability of computers. Prior to word-processing, the items in a list were numbered consecutively. This is still a good way of emphasizing details since it provides a way of separating details by importance and chronology.

The deliveries have been unsatisfactory in four ways:

1) They have been late.

2) They have not been scheduled.

3) They have not been recorded.

4) They have not been coordinated.

CAPITALS AND SMALL CAPITALS

Capitalizing the occasional word is another way to give emphasis to a word or phrase. Complete sentences should never be capitalized in business correspondence; it's too glaring. E-mail addresses that require capitalization are an exception to this rule.

The ability to print letters as "small capitals" is an interesting feature included in some word-processing software. The advantage is that words typed in lower case can be converted to small capitals by highlighting them and clicking the appropriate format item. Small caps look impressive when used as subheadings.

JUSTIFICATION

Justification determines how the words line up on the page. Left justification means that the words are flush with the left margin but appear uneven or ragged on the right. Since this was how most typed documents appeared in the past, it is felt that people are most comfortable with left justification. Center and right justification are irrelevant for basic letter and memo writing. Full justification means that all the words appear flush with the left side and the right side of the page. While this would seem to look as neat and clean as a book page, it rarely comes out that way on a simple word-processed document. Best to stick with left justification and a ragged-right margin.

CHAPTER FOURTEEN

Storing and retrieving your files

STORING HARD COPIES OF LETTERS AND FAXES

A small business or home office will soon accumulate a large quantity of correspondence. It becomes important to be able to store and retrieve these files without too much fuss. Even in small companies or home offices, it sometimes becomes necessary for someone other than the creator to retrieve a file.

Notwithstanding the wonderful powers of computers, paper is still with us for the foreseeable future. Hard copies - documents on paper - have the advantage of permanence that computer files do not. Upgraded versions of operating systems and word-processing programs can make old files difficult or impossible to retrieve. Computer hard drives and floppy disks can be affected by electrical storms, magnetic forces and computer viruses. Any of these can wipe out your electronic files in milliseconds. For this reason, it's essential that you devise a system for storing hard copies of important correspondence.

Metal filing cabinets are an inexpensive way of storing communications files. The legal-width cabinet is most commonly used since it allows for storage of both letter and legal-size documents. Most businesses use only legal-size file folders for the same reason. If your correspondence files are small, the file drawer in most desks will hold about 50 folders. Another option is a credenza with file drawers. A handy and inexpensive way to store files is in a cardboard banker's box which can be purchased at your local office-supply store.

Items of correspondence can be organized in filing cabinets in different ways depending on the volume of items. Documents related to the same matter or company should be filed together in one folder and the folder labelled to indicate its contents. As the folder grows, the items can be subdivided, possibly creating separate file folders for the different parties in the main category. Hanging file folders can be a good way to cluster together a number of files that relate to the same topic. Eventually it may become necessary to dedicate an entire drawer to one issue, company or topic. The outside of the drawer can then be labelled for future reference.

STORING AND RETRIEVING DOCUMENTS ON A COMPUTER

In theory, the filing of correspondence on your hard drive should parallel the storing of files in metal filing cabinets. The reality, unfortunately, is that computer files are rarely as organized as hard copies.

When many files are dumped into one directory, it becomes a time-consuming task to scroll or search to find one file. It is also possible for one letter to be added to another in the same file *ad infinitum.* The file gets so large that it takes forever to load and forever to find the specific letter or memo. Here are a few suggestions for the orderly storage and retrieval of correspondence on a computer:

- Separate work files from home or personal files.
- Create separate folders or directories for separate customers, clients or projects.
- Use a separate file name for each document.
- Backup hard disk files to a tape or floppy disk.

There are only three rules for making sure your computer files will always be available for your use: backup, backup, backup. Since everyone violates rule one and rule two, try to remember rule three once a week or so.

CHAPTER FIFTEEN

Master checklist for a great letter

- I have chosen an appropriate paper and matching envelope.
- I have set my margins so my letter will appear centered.
- I have decided on a format for this letter.
- I have dated the letter.
- I have spelled the recipient's name correctly.
- I have considered whether or not to use a subject line.
- I have considered the recipient before I selected a salutation.
- I have thought about the tone I want the letter to convey.
- I have thought about the effect my letter will have on the reader, myself and my company.
- I have used an introductory sentence or paragraph to begin my letter.
- I have used separate paragraphs to discuss each detail of the main topic.
- I have used a closing sentence or paragraph to convey my expectations to the reader.
- I have chosen the appropriate closing for the level of formality.
- I have copied the relevant parties.
- I have used the "Encl." line if I am enclosing documents.
- I have checked the grammar and spelling in this letter.
- I have used bullets, headings and sub-headings.
- I have enhanced the graphical appearance of the letter with bolding, font size, etc.
- I have not used profanity, vulgarity, racist or sexist language.
- **I am proud to sign my name to this letter.**

CHAPTER SIXTEEN

Sample letters, memos and faxes

JUDITH AMES, P.Eng.
24 Sussex Drive
Ottawa, Ontario K4E 19E
613-555-7697

April 16, 1997

Mr. Cam Embert
Personnel Manager
Acme Cheese Co. Ltd.
RR #2
Blyth, Ontario N0M 1

RE: CONSTRUCTION

Dear Sir:

I am enclosing my
advertisement for the
variety of projects incl
negotiating, troublesho
describes some of my

- tender, negotiate
- administer mont
- issue notices of
- schedule project programs;
- attend site meeti items;
- cooperate with
- use computers f

I would appreciate
answer any questions
personal interview.

Yours truly,

Judith Ames

Judith Ames, P.Eng.

JA/ja

Encl.

ACME CHEESE COMPANY

MEMO

Date: Marc

To: Mari

From: J.T. G

Subject: Late

The attached letter dat
pleased with the final
been a little rough on
over. I don't need to re
Grocers.

I'm suggesting we offe
leave the details up to

Distribution:
M. Ricotta
T. Pecorrino, F

ACME CHEESE CO.
R.R.#2, Blyth, Ontario N0M 1H0
(519) 555-1234 • Fax (519) 555-5678 • E-mail: office@cheeseco.ca

May 21, 1997

Judith Ames, P.Eng.
24 Sussex Dr.
Ottawa, Ontario
K4E 19E

Dear Ms. Ames:

Thank for your interest in the position of Construction Engineer, and for attending the interview on May 5th.

The interview team was very impressed with the high calibre of all the applicants and the final selection was not an easy one to make. We regret to advise you, however, that another applicant was selected to fill the position.

Thank you for your time and the best of luck to you in finding another position in the very near future.

Yours truly,

Cam Embert

Cam Embert
Personnel Manager

CE/jm

SAMPLE 1 –
JOB APPLICATION LETTER

JUDITH AMES, P.Eng.
24 Sussex Drive
Ottawa, Ontario K4E 19E
613-555-7697

April 16, 1997

Mr. Cam Embert
Personnel Manager
Acme Cheese Co. Ltd.
RR #2
Blyth, Ontario N0M 1H0

Re: **CONSTRUCTION ENGINEER POSITION**

Dear Sir:

I am enclosing my resume regarding your Globe and Mail advertisement for the above position. My consulting assignments cover a variety of projects including project management, safety, litigation, negotiating, troubleshooting and project completion. The following list describes some of my abilities which may be of value to you:

- tender, negotiate and let contracts to subcontractors;
- administer monthly progress draws;
- issue notices of change;
- schedule projects and monitor costs using a variety of computer programs;
- attend site meetings when necessary and follow up on "difficult" items;
- cooperate with other consultants involved in projects;
- use computers for the usual business needs.

I would appreciate an opportunity to elaborate on the above and answer any questions about my suitability for the position during a personal interview.

Yours truly,

Judith Ames

Judith Ames, P.Eng.

JA/ja

Encl.

SAMPLE 1 – DISCUSSION

STYLE:	Full block which is appropriate for a formal letter.
TONE:	Professional – persuasive – organized.
FORMALITY:	Formal. This is a letter from a professional engineer applying for a senior position; therefore formality is appropriate. Note the use of the title P.Eng. to reinforce the suitability of the writer for the position.
SUBJECT LINE:	The subject line reinforces the formal tone of the letter. The letter is being sent to a large organization, and the subject line helps direct the letter.
SALUTATION:	"Dear Sir:" to reinforce the formal tone of the letter.
TOPIC:	The purpose of the letter is to obtain an interview, not to get the job. If you are writing this kind of letter, refrain from going on and on about your qualifications. If you get to the interview stage, you'll have the chance to impress.
BEGINNING:	The introductory paragraph is straight to the point – the writer is interested in a job. The last sentence of the first paragraph leads to the middle section of the letter, the list of abilities.
MIDDLE:	Although not a paragraph in the real sense of the word, the list serves the same purpose: it gives details. A list suggests an organized mind, appropriate for an engineering position.
END:	The closing sentence states the real purpose of the letter, to get to the interview stage.
CLOSING:	"Yours truly," for a formal letter.
EFFECT:	This letter gives the recipient the impression of a straightforward, professional, organized person. Provided that the résumé backs up the letter, it should result in an interview.
SPECIAL POINTS:	The use of a list is an excellent idea for this type of letter. Note the colon at the end of the last sentence of the first paragraph. This prepares the reader for a list. The use of the bullets is an attractive way to set off each point in the list. The prepared by line "JA/ja" shows that the writer typed the letter herself, and since it is a businesslike document with some special enhancements, it shows the writer knows how to use a computer for word processing. This has become a criteria even for senior positions. The "Encl." line confirms that the résumé is included in the envelope.

SAMPLE 2 –
LETTER TO UNSUCCESSFUL JOB APPLICANT

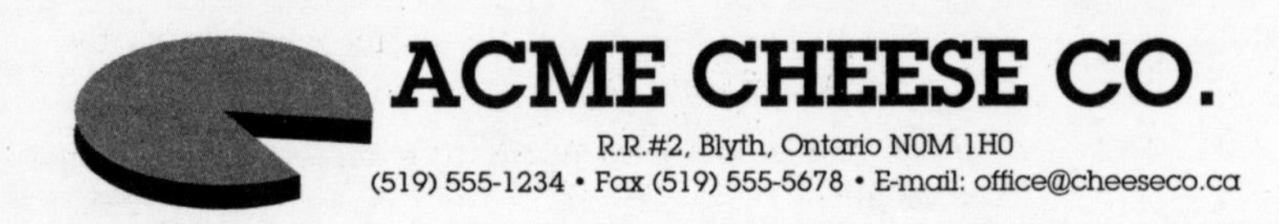

May 21, 1997

Judith Ames, P.Eng.
24 Sussex Dr.
Ottawa, Ontario
K4E 19E

Dear Ms. Ames:

Thank for your interest in the position of Construction Engineer, and for attending the interview on May 5th.

The interview team was very impressed with the high calibre of all the applicants and the final selection was not an easy one to make. We regret to advise you, however, that another applicant was selected to fill the position.

Thank you for your time and the best of luck to you in finding another position in the very near future.

Yours truly,

Cam Embert

Cam Embert
Personnel Manager

CE/jm

SAMPLE 2 – DISCUSSION

STYLE:	Full block.
TONE:	This is a bad-news letter but the writer wants to let the recipient down softly.
FORMALITY:	The letter is from a person holding a higher position than the recipient. The tone is formal, consoling, but final.
SUBJECT LINE:	Unless it a legal or official letter, the subject line is not necessary in letters to individuals who usually receive relatively small quantities of mail. A subject line here might seem too institutional.
SALUTATION:	Uses the person's last name. The individuals have met only once.
TOPIC:	The purpose of the letter is to inform Ms. Ames that she didn't get the job.
BEGINNING:	The introductory sentence is straight to the point. "Thank you" begins the letdown.
MIDDLE:	The second paragraph continues the soft letdown. Note the key words "impressed" and "regret." Some companies now make it a policy to include the name of the successful job applicant.
END:	The closing sentence offers best wishes.
CLOSING:	"Yours truly," for a formal letter.
EFFECT:	The reader will probably be disappointed, but at least she has been let down softly.
SPECIAL POINTS:	Note how concise this letter is. It is inappropriate to carry on at length with such a message.

SAMPLE 3 –
LETTER REQUESTING AN INTERVIEW

Harry Smally
251 Caroline Street
Wellford, Saskatchewan S3M 2U2
704-555-1234

February 28, 1999

Mr. Cam Embert
Personnel Manager
Acme Cheese Company Ltd.
RR #2, Blyth, Ontario
N0M 1H0

Re: **Position of Plant Manager**

Dear Mr. Embert:

I am writing regarding the position of Plant Manager advertised in the Blyth Herald on February 20, 1999. My résumé is enclosed for your reference.

My current position as Assistant Plant Manager at Shredded Cheese Co. Ltd. has given me the training to progress to the next level of management. Unfortunately, the Plant Manager position at Shredded will not be vacant for the foreseeable future. My present employer is aware of my intention to seek advancement outside the company.

At your convenience, I would like to schedule an interview. I will be at the Cheese Conference in Toronto from March 2-5. If you wish to contact me, I will be staying at the Four Seasons Hotel on Avenue Rd.

Yours sincerely,

Harry Smally

Harry Smally

HS/jk

Encl.

SAMPLE 3 – DISCUSSION

STYLE:	Full block.
TONE:	Businesslike.
FORMALITY:	Semiformal. Mr. Smally is already a part of upper management. He wishes to convey that point by maintaining a level of formality.
SUBJECT LINE:	Once again the subject line focuses the reader's attention.
SALUTATION:	Uses the person's last name; this is normal between two relative equals.
TOPIC:	The purpose of the letter is to schedule an interview.
BEGINNING:	The introductory sentence is straight to the point. The writer states the reason he is writing. He also indicates where he heard about the job.
MIDDLE:	The middle section provides some details of Mr. Smally's experience that may spark the reader's interest. Hopefully it will lead to the reading of the resumé.
END:	The closing paragraph uses the request words "at your convenience" and "if you wish." The reader is told where and when he can contact the writer.
CLOSING:	"Yours sincerely," for a semiformal letter.
EFFECT:	The reader should be reasonably impressed and give Mr. Smally an interview.
SPECIAL POINTS:	A résumé is included; therefore "Encl." is used.
	"HS/jk" shows that someone besides Mr. Smally typed the letter, a suggestion that he has staff people available to do this kind of task.
	The words in the subject line are bolded and underlined. Since this is the only typographical enhancement on the page, it stands out.

SAMPLE 4 – INVITATION TO SECOND INTERVIEW AND REQUEST FOR REFERENCES

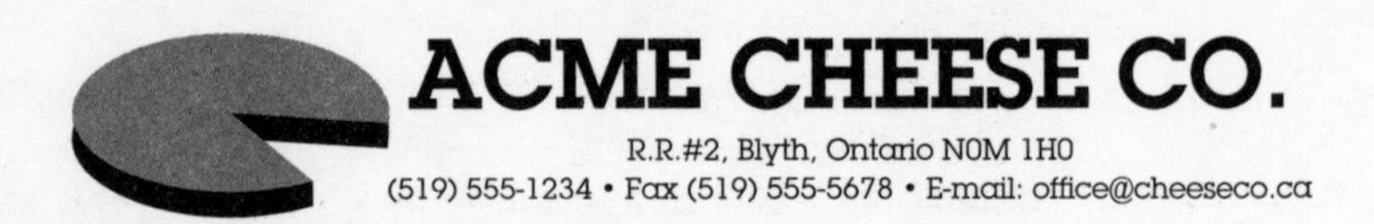

April 1, 1999

Mr. Harry Smally
251 Caroline St.
Wellford, Saskatchewan
S3M 2U2

Dear Mr. Smally:

Our hiring committee was impressed with you during the first phase of the interview process. We wish to invite you to a second interview on May 1 at 10:00 AM.

Before proceeding to the next interview level we require two references from business associates. These references should include name, address and telephone number of the referee and the duration and nature of your relationship. Each reference will be contacted by us before your next interview.

We look forward to our next meeting.

Yours sincerely,

Cam Embert

Cam Embert
Personnel Manager

CE/ms

SAMPLE 4 – DISCUSSION

STYLE:	Semi-block for less formality, although full block would be acceptable.
TONE:	Friendly - businesslike - encouraging - persuasive - to the point.
FORMALITY:	Semiformal. This is a letter from a company who is interested in the recipient as a prospective employee. The goal is to avoid the coldness of a formal tone but maintain a businesslike approach.
SUBJECT LINE:	The subject line is not necessary in faxes to individuals who usually receive relatively small quantities of mail. A subject line here might seem cold.
SALUTATION:	Uses the person's last name; this reinforces the businesslike tone of the letter.
TOPIC:	The purpose of the letter is to get the reader to submit references and come to another interview. The use of the words "impressed," "wish to invite," and "look forward to" encourages the writer to respond.
BEGINNING:	The introductory paragraph is straight to the point. The words "would appreciate" make it a polite request, not a demand.
MIDDLE:	The middle section provides the details for the required references.
END:	The closing sentence is a further way of encouraging the reader. It finishes the letter on a positive note.
CLOSING:	"Yours sincerely," for a semiformal letter.
EFFECT:	Provided that the reader is still interested in the position, and can supply the references, a positive response should be forthcoming.
SPECIAL POINTS:	The use of a friendly, positive tone should elicit a positive response. A concise expression of the requirements for references leaves no room for misunderstanding.

SAMPLE 5 – LETTER CHECKING REFERENCE FROM PREVIOUS EMPLOYER

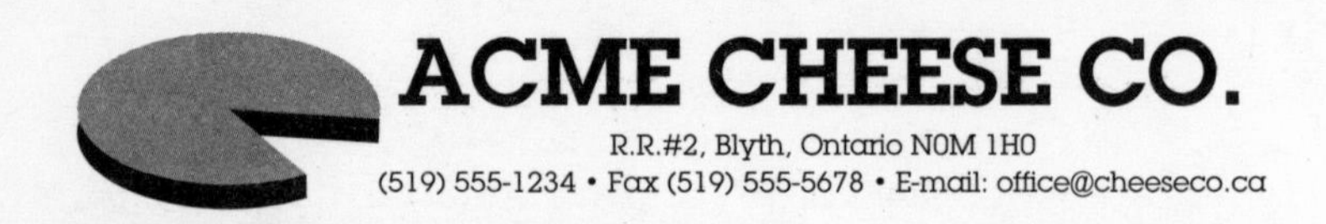

April 15, 1999

Personnel Manger
Cheddar Cheese Co.
989 Apple Street
Wellford, Saskatchewan
S4M 2A2

Subject: **Reference for Harry Smally**

A former employee of yours, Mr. Harry Smally, has applied for a position in our company. He gave your name as a reference. We would appreciate your cooperation in confirming the details of his employment history.

If possible we would like to know the beginning and end dates of Mr. Smally's employment, his final salary, a short description of his duties, and any comments you may have about his work at your company.

Thank you in advance for your cooperation.

Yours truly,

Cam Embert

Cam Embert
Personnel Manager

CE/ms

SAMPLE 5 – DISCUSSION

STYLE:	Simplified block; there is no salutation.
TONE:	Professional - to the point.
FORMALITY:	Formal. This is a letter from one personnel department to another.
SUBJECT LINE:	The subject line is essential since there is no salutation. The letter is being sent to a large organization, and the subject line helps direct the letter.
SALUTATION:	No salutation is used here because the writer does not know the name or gender of the recipient. When the salutation is absent, the subject line becomes mandatory.
TOPIC:	The purpose of the letter is pure information. This communication is between two middle-management people. There is no beating around the bush, just a straightforward request.
BEGINNING:	The introductory paragraph is straight and to the point. The words "would appreciate" make for a polite request, not a demand. The last sentence of the first paragraph leads to the first sentence of the middle section of the letter.
MIDDLE:	The middle section provides the details - exactly what information is being requested.
END:	The closing sentence is a polite way of saying Mr. Embert expects to receive the information as a matter of course.
CLOSING:	"Yours truly," for a formal letter.
EFFECT:	Cooperation between personnel managers is a foregone conclusion; therefore the required information should be produced without delay.

SAMPLE 6 –
OFFER OF EMPLOYMENT

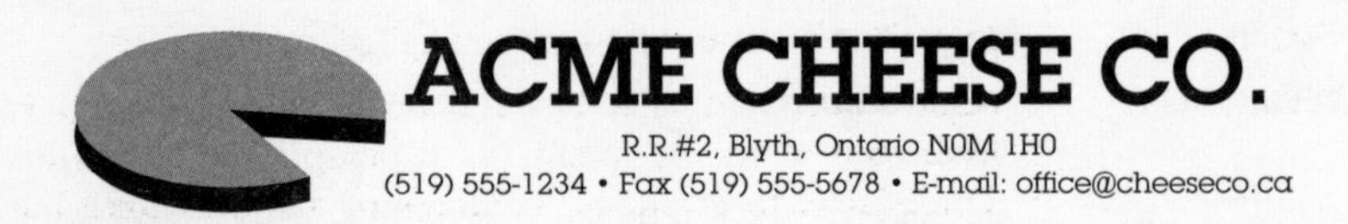

April 10, 1999

Mr. Harry Smally
251 Caroline St.
Wellford, Saskatchewan
S3M 2U2

Dear Mr. Smally:

We are pleased to give you written confirmation of our job offer for the position of Plant Manager.

The terms of the offer are as follows: starting salary of $80,000 per annum, a company car, plus our standard benefits package for which we have enclosed a brochure. The proposed starting date is April 30, 1999.

In the event that you accept the position, you will be eligible to participate in our stock option plan. This is a standard benefit we offer all our senior management personnel. We believe you will find the details of this plan attractive. A booklet is enclosed.

We require a response to this offer by April 15, 1999. The executive committee is anxious for you to join our team; therefore we look forward to your response.

Yours sincerely,

Cam Embert

Cam Embert
Personnel Manager

CE/ms

Encl. (2)

SAMPLE 6 – DISCUSSION

STYLE:	Full block.
TONE:	Friendly - businesslike - encouraging.
FORMALITY:	Semiformal. This is a letter from a company who is interested in the recipient as a prospective employee. The goal is to avoid the coldness of a formal tone but maintain an appropriate, professional distance. After all, Harry Smally might still turn down the job.
SUBJECT LINE:	The subject line is not necessary in letters to individuals who usually receive relatively small quantities of mail. A subject line here might seem too institutional.
SALUTATION:	Uses the person's last name; this reinforces the formal tone of the letter.
TOPIC:	The purpose of the letter is get to the reader to accept the job offer.
BEGINNING:	The introductory sentence is straight to the point. The word "pleased" emphasizes the friendly tone.
MIDDLE:	The first paragraph of the middle section provides the details and terms of employment. The second paragraph is a "hook," a persuasive device to add further inducement for the reader to accept the job.
END:	The first sentence of the closing paragraph sets limits on the reader that could induce an quick response. The key word is "require."
CLOSING:	"Yours sincerely," for a semiformal letter.
EFFECT:	If the applicant wants the job, he must respond within the time frame.
SPECIAL POINTS:	Two brochures are included; therefore "Encl." is used.

SAMPLE 7 –
WELCOME TO THE COMPANY

ACME CHEESE CO.

R.R.#2, Blyth, Ontario N0M 1H0
(519) 555-1234 • Fax (519) 555-5678 • E-mail: office@cheeseco.ca

---

April 24, 1999

Mr. Harry Smally
123 Oak Street
Blyth, Ontario
N0M 1H0

Dear Mr. Smally:

Welcome to Acme Cheese Co.! We're delighted that you've joined the Acme team.

We hope you'll feel at home here. The enclosed brochure will answer any questions you may have about policies and benefits at Acme.

If there are any further questions, please feel free to contact me anytime at ext. 223.

Yours sincerely,

Cam Embert

Cam Embert
Personnel Manager

CE/ms

Encl.

SAMPLE 7 – DISCUSSION

STYLE:	Semi-block, although some people prefer to use full block for both formal and semiformal correspondence.
TONE:	Friendly - feel good - warm.
FORMALITY:	Semiformal. The personnel manager hasn't developed a relationship with the new employee, and the semiformal tone is appropriate between an administrative manager and an employee.
SUBJECT LINE:	Is not required for this kind of letter; it would be too formal.
SALUTATION:	Uses the person's last name. Although Mr. Embert probably met Mr. Smally at the job interview, use of the last name is common as a gesture of respect. At some point, perhaps after another meeting or two, they can correspond as Cam and Harry.
TOPIC:	The topic is a simple, enthusiastic welcome to the company.
BEGINNING:	The introductory, two-sentence paragraph jumps off the page. It leaves no doubt about the reason for the letter.
MIDDLE:	Another two-sentence paragraph: the first reinforces the welcome message, the second is information about the enclosure of the brochure.
END:	The closing sentence reinforces the welcome theme by giving the new employee access to the personnel manager. Note the use of the positive phrase "please feel free to contact me."
CLOSING:	"Yours sincerely," for a semiformal letter.
EFFECT:	This letter should give the employee a positive feeling about the new company. It's friendly, helpful and welcoming.
SPECIAL POINTS:	The positive use of the exclamation mark gives an exuberant flavour to the first line. The "Encl." line confirms that something has been included in the envelope.

SAMPLE 8 –
LETTER OF RECOMMENDATION

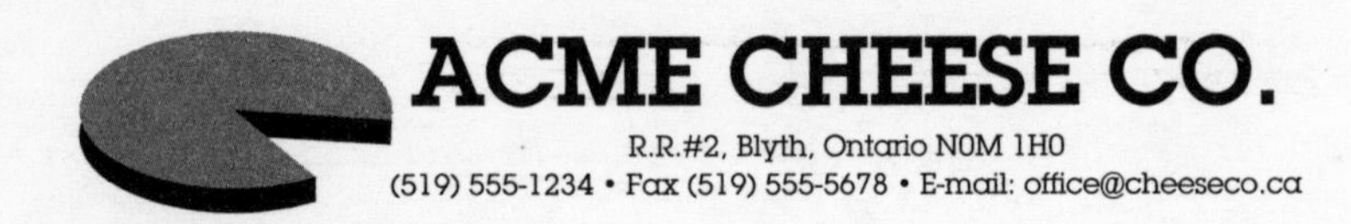

November 28, 1999

Ideal Fudge Company Limited
Ms. Nancy Albright
Personnel Manager
PO Box 123
Gimble, Saskatchewan
M1M 2Z2

Re: **Recommendation for Paul Smith**

Dear Ms. Albright:

Paul Smith worked for Acme Cheese Company for six years, from Jan. 12, 1993 to Jan. 23, 1999.

Paul was an excellent employee; he was always on time and put in a good day's work. We checked our records and found that Paul had only missed 10 days' work over the five years he worked here. Paul carried out the tasks we set for him efficiently, although he did not show any particular desire for advancement.

It is an unfortunate fact that in times of slow business, companies are often forced to downsize. Due to seniority provisions in our union agreement, Paul had to be laid off. This did not reflect on his value as an employee, and we would be happy to rehire him if business picked up. It is therefore our pleasure to recommend Paul to anyone looking for a hard-working employee.

Yours sincerely,

Cam Embert

Cam Embert
Personnel Manager

CE/ms

SAMPLE 8 – DISCUSSION

STYLE:	Full block.
TONE:	Businesslike - to the point.
FORMALITY:	Semiformal. The sender and receiver are equals.
SUBJECT LINE:	The subject line is useful for busy offices and managers.
SALUTATION:	Uses the person's last name; this is normal between two equals.
TOPIC:	The purpose of the letter is to give a recommendation for a former employee. A letter of recommendation that is full of too much praise would not be credible. This is the reason for the inclusion of the last sentence in the middle paragraph..
BEGINNING:	The introductory sentence is straight to the point. It could be joined to the second paragraph, but it emphasizes the six-year stretch of employment.
MIDDLE:	The positive work history details are qualified in the last sentence.
END:	The closing paragraph explains why Paul isn't working at Acme Cheese anymore. The words "pleasure" and "hard-working" reinforce the positive message of the letter.
CLOSING:	"Yours sincerely," for a semiformal letter.
EFFECT:	The reader is given a favourable view of Mr. Smith.
SPECIAL POINTS:	The words in the subject line are capitalized, bolded and underlined. Since this is the only typographical enhancement other than the letterhead, it stands out.

SAMPLE 9 –
LETTER OF COMMENDATION TO EMPLOYEE

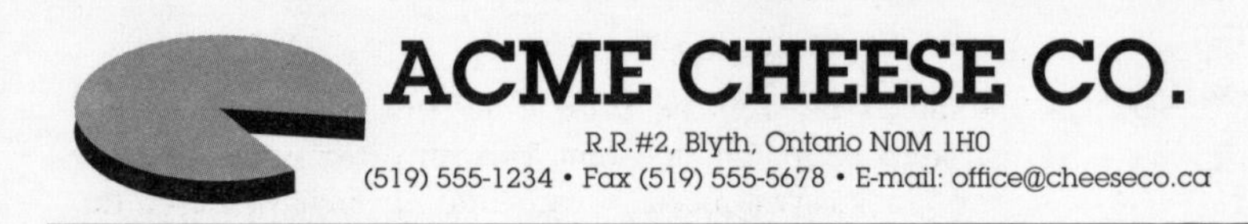
ACME CHEESE CO.
R.R.#2, Blyth, Ontario N0M 1H0
(519) 555-1234 • Fax (519) 555-5678 • E-mail: office@cheeseco.ca

October 14, 1999

Mr. Harry Smally
123 Oak St.
Blyth, Ontario
N0M 1H0

Dear ~~Mr. Smally~~: Harry

I would like to commend you for the work you did on the reorganization of the bulk cheese department. Your contribution was fundamental to the success of the project.

The extra care you gave this project was admirable, and I appreciate your vigilance on behalf of the company's interests.

I am proud to have you on the Acme team and proud of your work, particularly on the bulk cheese project. Thanks again for your efforts.

Yours sincerely,

J. T. Gouda

J.T. Gouda
President - Acme Cheese Co.

cc: Cam Embert, Personnel Manager

JG/ms

SAMPLE 9 – DISCUSSION

STYLE:	Full block; semi-block would be fine as well.
TONE:	Warm - good feeling.
FORMALITY:	Semiformal. This is from a person holding a higher position than the recipient, but the topic is friendly. A copy of this will make its way into Mr. Smally's file in the Personnel Department.
SUBJECT LINE:	Not necessary in a warm letter from the president of the company to one of his employees. Generally speaking, the subject line is not necessary in letters to individuals who usually receive relatively small quantities of mail. A subject line in this case would detract from the warm tone.
SALUTATION:	Uses the person's last name, as is appropriate in semiformal letters. The strike-over of the printed salutation personalizes the letter. This adds to the warm tone.
TOPIC:	The purpose of the letter is to give a commendation for good work.
BEGINNING:	The introductory sentence is straight to the point. It tells the "why" of the letter. The use of the first-person "I," as opposed to the corporate "we," adds to the personal warmth.
MIDDLE:	The second paragraph continues the good-news message with the use of "extra care," "admirable," "appreciate" and "vigilance."
END:	The closing paragraph reiterates the praise with the word "proud" mentioned twice, and the extra "thanks" in the last line.
CLOSING:	"Yours sincerely," for a semiformal letter.
EFFECT:	The reader is given credit for good work. These letters can be a great boost to employee morale.
SPECIAL POINTS:	Note the repeated use of the word "proud" in the first in the last paragraph. Parallel structures like this will hammer home a message.

SAMPLE 10 –
LETTER REQUESTING PAYMENT

February 13, 1999

Mr. John Smith
President
Grocers Company
7000 Rene Levesque Blvd. West
Montreal, Quebec H3B 1Y9

RE: **OVERDUE ACCOUNT**

Dear Sir:

Acme Cheese Co. Ltd. appreciates your business; however our accounts receivable department indicates that your account #345678 is overdue in the amount of $10,000.

We understand that mistakes happen and sometimes payments are overlooked. However, it is important that we receive your payment within 10 days. If you cannot meet this deadline, please call me directly at ext. 426.

If you have already sent the payment, please accept our apologies for this reminder. It is our fervent hope that we will be able to continue the excellent relationship we have had with you in the past.

Yours truly,

Maria Ricotta

Maria Ricotta (Mrs.)
Credit Manager

MR/ms

SAMPLE 10 – DISCUSSION

STYLE: Full block - this is a formal letter.

TONE: This is the first request for overdue payment, so the tone is businesslike but cordial.

FORMALITY: Formal.

SUBJECT LINE: Definitely a good idea here. It gets the letter attention - and directed quickly.

SALUTATION: "Dear Sir:" or "Dear Madam:" or similar variations are best to set the formal tone.

TOPIC: The purpose of the letter is to get a payment, or to find out why the payment is late.

BEGINNING: The introductory sentence is straight to the point. The use of "appreciates" in the first sentence establishes a cordial tone at the outset.

MIDDLE: The second paragraph continues with the cordial tone. Note the words "understand" and "overlooked." Key words in the next sentences - "important," "payment" and "deadline" - emphasize the serious nature of the letter.

END: The last line allows face-saving by giving the recipient an "out." Note the conditional "if" clause and the key words "please," "accept," "apologies," "fervent hope" and "excellent relationship."

CLOSING: "Yours truly," in keeping with the tone of a formal letter.

EFFECT: If the recipient is well intentioned, this kind of request will usually result in a payment. If it doesn't, then we go to Sample 11.

SPECIAL POINTS: The Grocers Company is located in Montreal, but Acme Cheese has decided to keep with standard English spelling for place names. The typist could also have opted for "Montréal, Québec." Often the letterhead of a Quebec company will indicate how they prefer the address to be handled.

Note the bolding and capitalization in the subject line. Since this is the first request for payment, it has a flavour of "We're sorry to mention it, but you owe us a pile of money. But if you've already sent it, we're sorry we asked."

SAMPLE 11 –
FOLLOW-UP LETTER REQUESTING PAYMENT

February 24, 1999

Mr. John Smith
President
Grocers Company
7000 Rene Levesque Blvd. West
Montreal, Quebec H3B 1Y9

RE: **OVERDUE ACCOUNT**

Dear Sir:

We refer you to our letter of February 13, 1999 in which we informed you of your overdue account #345678 and our request for payment. It is now past the 10-day period and we have not received your payment.

We have your next order packed and ready to ship; unfortunately, until we receive your overdue payment this shipment is on hold. Please contact this office by 12:00 noon February 28, 1999 to explain the arrangements for payment.

Yours truly,

Maria Ricotta (Mrs.)
Credit Manager

MR/ms

cc: J.T. Gouda - President - Acme Cheese Co.

SAMPLE 11 – DISCUSSION

STYLE:	Full block. This is a formal letter. It would be sent by courier.
TONE:	This is the second request for overdue payment, so the cordial tone of the first letter is gone. This letter is not nasty but has an "edge" to it. The writer should sound irritated.
FORMALITY:	Formal. This is a serious letter and calls for immediate action. This letter will become part of the paper trail should Acme Cheese have to go to court to obtain payment.
SUBJECT LINE:	Bolded, capitalized and underlined; it helps to emphasize the topic.
SALUTATION:	"Dear Sir:" or "Dear Madam:" is best for a formal tone.
TOPIC:	The purpose is to follow the first polite letter with a "pressure letter" to get payment or at least discussion on the issue.
BEGINNING:	The introductory sentence refers to the previous letter. This can be important if writing to a large firm; it is possible that the first letter was overlooked. Note the use of "overdue" and "not received."
MIDDLE:	The second paragraph contains a "pressure" statement - Acme's decision to delay shipment. Note the word "unfortunately" which subliminally says "this is your fault; we really don't want to be so tough." Even with the irritated edge, the word "please" maintains a polite, businesslike tone.
END:	The absence of a last line or paragraph emphasizes the curt tone of the letter - no niceties here.
CLOSING:	"Yours truly," in keeping with the tone of a formal letter.
EFFECT:	The reader should have no question about the mood of the writer. Aside from the real threat of suspended delivery, there is a "between the lines" tone of "pay up or else."
SPECIAL POINTS:	This is the second request for late payment. The real message is "We took the time to write you a nice letter to remind you about a late payment, but you ignored us. Now we're really upset, so you had better pay up immediately." The curtness adds to the irritated tone. Note that the letter is copied to the president of Acme Cheese. This is another way of emphasizing the seriousness of the matter.

SAMPLE 12 – REMITTANCE WITH APOLOGY FOR LATE PAYMENT

GROCERS COMPANY
7000 Rene Levesque Blvd. West
Montreal, Quebec H3B 1Y9

February 27, 1999

Mr. J.T. Gouda
President
Acme Cheese Co. Ltd.
RR #2, Blyth, Ontario
N0M 1H0

RE: **OVERDUE ACCOUNT**

Dear Sir:

Please accept our most profound apologies for the mix-up in payment of our account #345678.

We have enclosed two cheques. Cheque #4532 for $10,000 to bring our account up to date, and cheque #4533 for $5,000 which is an advance payment for our shipment that is sitting in your warehouse.

We certainly wish to maintain the excellent relationship we developed with you; therefore allow us to explain the reason why our account got so far behind. Our accounts payable manager has been on vacation for three weeks and the workload has been too much for her assistant. We are sure that things will be back to normal once our regular staff person returns tomorrow.

Once again, sorry for the delay.

Cordially yours,

John Smith

John Smith
President

JS/sm

SAMPLE 12 – DISCUSSION

STYLE:	Full block. This is a formal letter in response to a formal letter. It would be sent by courier.
TONE:	Apologetic and conciliatory.
FORMALITY:	Formal. This is a reply to a serious letter. A less formal style and tone might show disrespect for Acme Cheese's previous correspondence. Nonetheless, the writer eases up on the formal tone with the explanation offered.
SUBJECT LINE:	Bolded and capitalized. This helps to focus the reader on the topic.
SALUTATION:	"Dear Sir:" - the two presidents do not know each other.
TOPIC:	The purpose of the letter is to re-establish the relationship - and give a reason why the account was not paid.
BEGINNING:	The introductory sentence goes right to the heart of the matter. Note the use of "please accept" and "profound apologies."
MIDDLE:	The second paragraph contains the sugar-coating for the apology; two cheques, one an advance payment. The next paragraph of the middle section gives a reason for the late payment, however implausible it may be. Note the key words "wish," "excellent relationship" and "back to normal."
END:	The last line reiterates the apology.
CLOSING:	"Cordially yours," is less formal than the rest of the letter, but it works here because the phrase sends the message "OK, we messed up, but we gave you more money than we needed to, so now let's be buddies again."
EFFECT:	The apology is backed up by the cheques and a reason for being late. The recipient should be mollified, and ready to continue doing business with the tardy customer.
SPECIAL POINTS:	Note that the letter is addressed to the president of Acme Cheese. Mr. Smith obviously noted that the president had been copied on the second demand for payment.

SAMPLE 13 –
MEMO GIVING INSTRUCTIONS TO AN EMPLOYEE

ACME CHEESE COMPANY

MEMO

Date: March 10, 1999

To: Maria Ricotta

From: J.T. Gouda

Subject: Late payments by Grocers Company

The attached letter dated February 21 from Grocers is for your files. I'm pleased with the final result here and I accept their excuse. We may have been a little rough on them so I want you to write and smooth things over. I don't need to remind you that we do a lot of business with Grocers.

I'm suggesting we offer them an additional discount for early payment. I'll leave the details up to you.

Distribution:

M. Ricotta
T. Pecorrino, Finance

SAMPLE 13 – DISCUSSION

FORMAT:	Company memo form.
PURPOSE:	To give instructions to an employee.
TONE:	Informal and businesslike. The use of contractions underscores the familiar working relationship.
CONTENTS:	Mr. Gouda is dealing with a key person in his company. He is brief and to the point. He includes a copy of the letter because the original was not addressed or copied to Maria. His instructions are to the point. He is giving orders which he expects to be carried out. He obviously respects Maria enough to delegate the details of the discount to her.
SPECIAL POINTS:	Note the use of the first person pronoun "I." Business between companies is impersonal; therefore "we" is normally used. The correspondence between people who work within a company is usually more personal.

A few tips on effective memos:

- A memo sent in anger is like a bullet; it cannot be called back.
- Don't use acronyms unless you're sure every reader will understand them.
- Inappropriate informality can spoil an otherwise solid message.
- A pleasant, conversational tone often persuades best.
- Before posting the memo, put yourself in the shoes of the recipients. How would you feel about receiving such a memo?

SAMPLE 14 –
LETTER OF THANKS FOR REMITTANCE

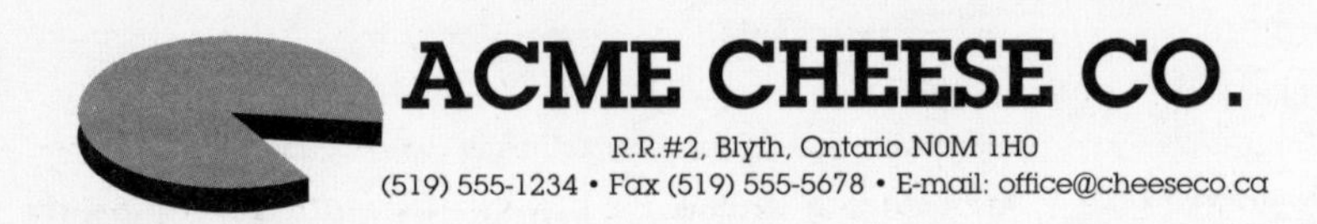

March 10, 1999

Mr. John Smith
President
Grocers Company
7000 Rene Levesque Blvd. West
Montreal, Quebec H3B 1Y9

FAXED ONLY

RE: **REMITTANCE**

Dear Sir:

Thank you for the cheques for $10,000 and $5,000.

We understand that there was an administrative mix-up in your accounts payable department. Your order has been sent out by express and you should receive it by tomorrow.

We are enclosing a copy of a revised policy which gives a 3% discount to our most valued customers, including Grocers Company, for payment within 10 days of delivery. We hope you will be able to make use of this discount in future orders from us.

Kindest regards,

Maria Ricotta

Maria Ricotta (Mrs.)
Credit Manager

Enclosure

MR/ms

SAMPLE 14 – DISCUSSION

STYLE:	Full block imparts formality to the resolution of a serious matter.
TONE:	Understanding, accepting and conciliatory.
FORMALITY:	Formal. This is the last volley in a series of formal letters.
SUBJECT LINE:	Bolded and capitalized; helps to focus the reader on the topic.
SALUTATION:	"Dear Sir:", "Dear Madam:" or similar variations are best to express a formal tone.
TOPIC:	The purpose of the letter is to accept the apology and confirm the re-establishment of the relationship. The discount serves both as a symbol and as a financial incentive for improved and speedier payment.
BEGINNING:	The simple, short introductory sentence stands out and says "You paid us, thanks."
MIDDLE:	This includes the acceptance of the reason for the late payment, and the reassurance that everything is back on track.
END:	The last sentence emphasizes the status of the Grocers Company with Acme Cheese and gives them a reason to pay on time in the future.
CLOSING:	"Kindest regards," is another example of how a letter might start with a formal tone and end less formally. The subliminal message is "You paid us, maybe we got a little too upset, but we've showed how understanding we can be."
EFFECT:	Everything should be back to normal between these two companies.
SPECIAL POINTS:	This faxed letter is from the credit manager rather than from the president. The between-the-lines message is that everything is back to normal, our middle manager is handling matters now, so don't worry about the long-term relationship. Also note the line FAXED ONLY. This has become more common with increased faxing of correspondence. A fax cover would not be necessary for this message since all the information is on the letter. Sometimes the line FAXED AND MAILED is inserted, especially if the letter may have some legal importance.

SAMPLE 15 –
LETTER REQUESTING A MEETING

April 20, 1999

Mr. John Henry
President
The Dofer Manufacturing Co. Ltd.
123 Cherry Street
Toronto, Ontario
M3C 2C2

Dear John,

I'm going to be in Toronto on April 30, and I'd like to meet with you if possible.

Morning is best for me. Would nine o'clock be convenient for you? I'd like to spend about two hours talking about the new pasteurizer.

If this fits your schedule, leave a message with my secretary. In any case I'll confirm the appointment before I arrive. Looking forward to seeing you.

Best regards,

Jack

John Gouda
President

JG/ms

SAMPLE 15 – DISCUSSION

STYLE:	Full block.
TONE:	Casual - informal - friendly.
FORMALITY:	Informal. This is a letter between well-acquainted executives.
SUBJECT LINE:	Not necessary.
SALUTATION:	"Dear John," - notice the comma rather than a colon.
TOPIC:	The desire to meet and discuss business.
BEGINNING:	Since there is no subject line, the first sentence states the topic.
MIDDLE:	Gives the details of possible meeting times.
END:	Confirms that a further communication is requested.
CLOSING:	"Best regards," conveys the personal informal relationship.
EFFECT:	Should lead to a return call or contact from the recipient.
SPECIAL POINTS:	In the past, a note like this was often mailed in advance of business trips. These days, a fax, voice-mail or possibly an E-mail message would be more likely. Nonetheless, this remains the format for a "between friends" business letter.

SAMPLE 16 –
LETTER OF INTENT

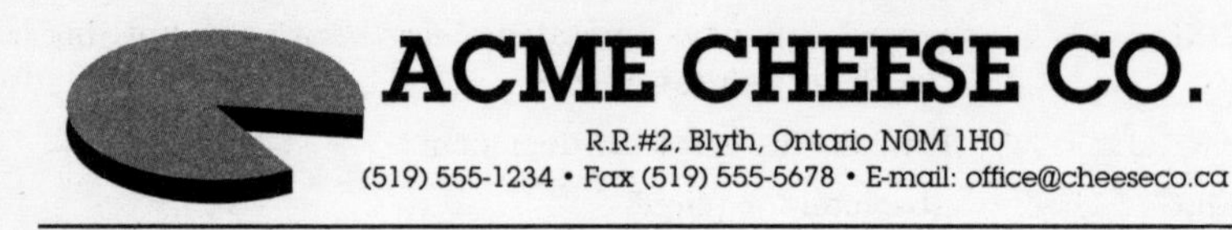

May 21, 1999

Mr. John Henry
President
The Dofer Manufacturing Co. Ltd.
123 Cherry St.
Toronto, Ontario
M3C 2C2

RE: LETTER OF INTENT

Dear Sir:

This letter will serve as notification of our intent to enter into a contract with The Dofer Manufacturing Co. Ltd. to supply Acme Cheese Co. Ltd. with a Model 100008-A pasteurizer.

The terms and conditions of this letter are based on the tender documents sent to you on Feb. 28, 1999, and on the bid you delivered to us on March 15, 1999. This letter of intent expires 10 days from today's date, and thereafter becomes null and void.

We look forward to your response and to a mutually profitable relationship between our companies.

Yours truly,

J.T. Gouda
President - Acme Cheese Co.

JG/ms

SAMPLE 16 – DISCUSSION

STYLE:	Full block.
TONE:	Formal - the two presidents may be friends, but this is strictly a business matter.
FORMALITY:	Formal. This is a legal document.
SUBJECT LINE:	Absolutely required.
SALUTATION:	"Dear Sir:" keeps it formal.
TOPIC:	The intent to form a contract.
BEGINNING:	The one-sentence paragraph states the specific topic.
MIDDLE:	Gives the details, the reference for the terms. This is the truly formal part of the letter and essential should there be any problem with the deal later on.
END:	Closes with a friendly, feel-good statement.
CLOSING:	"Yours truly," to maintain the formality.
EFFECT:	If signed and returned this letter is legally binding.
SPECIAL POINTS:	A letter of intent is used so that two businesses who intend to sign a contract can begin working together before the contract is signed. If the contract is later not signed, one or the other may use the letter of intent to sue for damages. Large companies use this type of letter often. If you are not familiar with a letter of intent, get some legal advice before writing or signing one.

SAMPLE 17 –
FAX / LETTER OF DELAY

ACME CHEESE CO.

R.R.#2, Blyth, Ontario N0M 1H0
(519) 555-1234 • Fax (519) 555-5678 • E-mail: office@cheeseco.ca

---

Aug. 21, 1999

Mr. John Henry
President
The Dofer Manufacturing Co. Ltd.
123 Cherry St.
Toronto, Ontario
M3C 2C2

WITHOUT PREJUDICE

RE: DELAY IN DELIVERY OF PASTEURIZER

FAXED AND MAILED

Dear Sir:

We wish to inform you that there has been a delay in the shipment of the Model 100008-A pasteurizer.

The terms of the contract between us specifies that the pasteurizer was to be delivered no later than Aug. 18, 1999. There has been **no** delivery. If there is a reason for the delay, please advise us. We also wish to know if there is a revised delivery date.

If we incur damages due to further delay in delivering the pasteurizer, we will advise you of them. We also wish to remind you of the penalty clause of $100.00 per day for failure to deliver on time.

Please respond immediately on this matter.

Yours truly,

J. T. Gouda

J.T. Gouda
President - Acme Cheese Co.

JG/ms

SAMPLE 17 – DISCUSSION

STYLE:	Full block.
TONE:	Formal - legalistic - unfriendly. This kind of letter might be called a "shake 'em up" letter.
FORMALITY:	Formal. This communication could be used in future litigation.
SUBJECT LINE:	Absolutely required. Note that this letter is marked "FAXED AND MAILED," the former for speed, the latter for legal reasons.
SALUTATION:	"Dear Sir:" keeps it formal. The two presidents were friends, but the shipment's delay makes even that dicey.
TOPIC:	Delay with possible legal ramifications.
BEGINNING:	The one-sentence paragraph becomes more important in documents that may be used in court. It leaves no ambiguity about the topic.
MIDDLE:	Two paragraphs give the details, the reference for the delay. The writer wishes to indicate that he knows he is on sure ground and to advise the recipient of the consequences. Note the bolding of the word "no."
END:	Closes with a demand for a response.
CLOSING:	"Yours truly," to maintain the formality.
EFFECT:	Gets attention. Should result in some kind of response. Any company that ignored this kind of letter would be foolish indeed.
SPECIAL POINTS	It is an unfortunate fact that many business relationships end up, if not in court, at least in potential lawsuits. The quality of letters used to support litigation has a direct bearing on the outcome. Courts frown on extraneous, frivolous material in letters presented to support a legal action. The material must be organized, the language plain and to the point. A collection of letters is called a "paper trail," another good reason to have an excellent filing system. It is a good idea to keep "hard copies" of important letters in addition to the ones on your computer, and also to backup letters from the hard disk to a floppy disk. Note the words "WITHOUT PREJUDICE." This means that no matter what you write in a letter, it will have no effect on past, present or future claims or actions that are ongoing or about to happen. Ask your lawyer about inserting these words on letters related to legal matters.

SAMPLE 18 –
LETTER THREATENING LEGAL ACTION

Sept. 11, 1999

Mr. John Henry **WITHOUT PREJUDICE**
President
The Dofer Manufacturing Co. Ltd.
123 Cherry St.
Toronto, Ontario
M3C 2C2

RE: LEGAL ACTION RELATED TO FAILURE TO DELIVER PASTEURIZER

Dear Sir:

Since we contracted with you to supply a Model 100008-A pasteurizer to us, the series of events has unfortunately evolved to the point where you leave us no choice but to initiate legal proceedings.

The basis for this decision is explained as follows:

- The contract stipulates that the pasteurizer was to be delivered on or before Aug. 18, 1999. You did not do this.
- We wrote to you on August 21, 1999 regarding the delay. Your letter of Aug. 24, 1999 did not explain the reason for the delay or confirm a revised delivery date.
- Your failure to deliver the pasteurizer as agreed in the contract has caused a loss of production and profit.

The terms of the contract include a penalty clause. We intend to invoke that clause. The calculation of our other damages will follow in subsequent correspondence. We did not want to embark on this course but see no other recourse. If there is any way you feel we can avoid this legal action, please call us to discuss a possible resolution.

Yours truly,

J. J. Gouda

John Gouda
President - Acme Cheese Co. Ltd.

JG/ms
cc: Mr. Burnside, Barrister and Solicitor

SAMPLE 18 – DISCUSSION

STYLE:	Full block.
TONE:	Formal - legalistic - the final "shake 'em up" letter.
FORMALITY:	Formal. This could well be used in future litigation. Of course, it is never wise to threaten legal action unless you intend to proceed with it. In this case, the next step is clear.
SUBJECT LINE:	Absolutely required.
SALUTATION:	"Dear Sir:" keeps it formal.
TOPIC:	Threat of legal action.
BEGINNING:	The first paragraph revisits the history. It leaves no ambiguity about the topic. The key words are "unfortunately" and "you leave us no choice." This emphasizes who is the aggrieved party.
MIDDLE:	The list organizes the facts. Note the use of bullets.
END:	This is a "good cop - bad cop" routine. In the first four sentences the writer lists the possible consequences; in the last sentence he pulls back with the possibility of reconciliation.
CLOSING:	Formal.
EFFECT:	Once again, an attention-getter. This should result in a response. Any company that ignored this kind of letter deserves to end up in court.
SPECIAL POINTS:	Note the inclusion of the words WITHOUT PREJUDICE, and that the writer has copied his lawyer. This is sometimes done to intimidate rather than begin legal action. These kinds of letters are relatively common in some industries; they usually result in a resolution before the situation actually involves lawyers.

SAMPLE 19 – LETTER OF APOLOGY AND RECONCILIATION

THE DOFER MANUFACTURING CO. LTD.
123 Cherry St., Toronto, ON. M3C 2C2

Sept. 15, 1999

Mr. J.T. Gouda
President
Acme Cheese Company Limited
RR #2 Blyth, Ontario
N0M 1H0

WITHOUT PREJUDICE

RE: PASTEURIZER MODEL 100008-A

Dear Sir:

We realize that there has been some difficulty in filling your order for the above piece of equipment, and we wish to apologize for any trouble this may have caused you. We acknowledge receipt of your letters of August 21 and September 11, 1999, and cannot dispute the facts described therein. We wish, however, to point out several mitigating factors:

- We have had a strike at our plant since August 1, 1999. This is a factor beyond our control; therefore we cannot be held responsible for the impact it might have on your operation.
- It is also true that your old pasteurizer is still operating. A minor delay in shipment should not greatly affect your manufacturing costs or capacity.

We have always had a good relationship with Acme over the years. We intend to make sure that our relationship gets back on track. We expect to be able to deliver the pasteurizer by October 15, 1999. Because we value your business, we are going to give you a five-year extension of the warranty free of charge. Please contact me personally if you have any further concerns.

Yours truly,

John Henry - President

JH/gk

cc: Susan Bonhomme
Spring, Wing & Bonhomme, Barristers and Solicitors

SAMPLE 19 – DISCUSSION

STYLE:	Full block.
TONE:	Apologetic - formal - legalistic - businesslike.
FORMALITY:	Formal. This could be used in litigation if Acme refuses to accept the apology and continues to press for damages.
SUBJECT LINE:	Absolutely required.
SALUTATION:	"Dear Sir:" keeps it formal.
TOPIC:	An apology with an explanation and an offer of reconciliation.
BEGINNING:	The first paragraph admits responsibility for the problem. The last sentence modifies this admission.
MIDDLE:	Two bulleted points that detail the "mitigating factors."
END:	A promise of delivery and an inducement to bring the relationship back to normal.
CLOSING:	"Yours truly," for formality.
EFFECT:	The acceptance of responsibility, the inclusion of mitigating reasons and the conciliatory tone should resolve the matter.
SPECIAL POINTS:	Again note the inclusion of the words "WITHOUT PREJUDICE," and that the writer has copied his lawyer. Mr. Henry is saying, "I'm not scared because you copied your lawyer, I'm copying mine!" The most notable aspect of this letter is its reasonable tone which goes a long way toward resolving issues. If this matter gets to court, the judge will look favourably on Mr. Henry's reasonable attitude.

SAMPLE 20 –
FAX TO ACCOUNTS PAYABLE

FAX TRANSMISSION

Date: September 21, 2010

Number of pages including this one (5)

To: Peter Smith
Accounts Payable Manager
Grocers Company
7000 Rene Levesque Blvd. West
Montreal, Quebec H3B 1Y9

From: Maria Ricotta
Credit Manager

Subject: Packing slips for invoices
#345234, #345235, #345236, #345237

As you requested, we are faxing copies of these packing slips so that you can correlate them with our invoices. You will note that the shipments were signed and dated by Mary Morgan in your shipping department. If there is a problem, please call me directly at ext. 231.

SAMPLE 20 – DISCUSSION

FORMAT:	Preprinted company fax form.
PURPOSE:	To send copies of packing slips.
TONE:	Businesslike. The tone is neutral since the fax is merely a response to a request for copies. Once the copies have been supplied, there may be no further communication on this matter.
CONTENTS:	The writer makes the point that the slips were signed and dated by an employee of Grocers Company, a point Peter Smith will be sure to check. She also makes sure that he can reach her by phone if there is a problem.
SPECIAL POINTS:	Since this is a preprinted company form, it is unnecessary to repeat the sender's address in the "From:" line.

SAMPLE 21 –
MEMO ANNOUNCING A NEW POLICY

ACME CHEESE COMPANY

MEMO

Date: May 21, 1997

To: All employees

From: John Gouda

Subject:: **New policy on absenteeism**

As we all know, the recent downsizing of our workforce has placed a greater responsibility on each of us to do our jobs. In the past, if any of us had to take time off work, we were able to fill in with other employees. This is no longer the case.

After investigating the reasons for absenteeism, we find that conflicts between work and family responsibilities are one of the primary causes for people to "call in sick." With this in mind the company has instituted a system of flextime. Those employees who wish to vary their work schedule may confer with their department heads and come up with an arrangement acceptable to all parties.

Distribution: Bulletin board
All department heads

SAMPLE 21 – DISCUSSION

FORMAT: Preprinted company memo form.

PURPOSE: To circulate a new policy.

TONE: Businesslike and somewhat formal. This is a corporate memo from the executive to the employees. The word "we" gives a tone of "we're all in this downsizing mess together."

CONTENTS: This is a "bad news - good news" memo. The company is saying, "There is a problem but we have a solution." There are two paragraphs, one for the problem and one for the solution.

SPECIAL POINTS: Note the posting of the memo on the company bulletin board.

Correspondence Summary

When to send . . .

A letter.	When speed is not essential. When privacy matters. When a legal problem is possible (special delivery or confirmed receipt is a good idea).
A fax.	When privacy doesn't matter and speed does.
A memo.	For internal communication. Best for short notes and general policy items.
E-mail.	For short communications. Neither speed nor privacy are assured.

Addresses . . .

The postal code *in the inside address* is on the line after the city and province.

The postal code *on the envelope* must come on the same line as the city and province.

Addresses in Quebec can be written in either French or English, but should be handled consistently. A good approach is to follow the language used on the Quebec firm's letterhead.

Postal codes are not optional. Canada Post charges extra to deliver a letter without a postal code. The American postal system will sometimes just return such a letter to the sender.

On your computer . . .

- Use the "Wizard" function to help format your letter.
- Remember to date the letter the day it's written, not the print date.
- Remember that the computer spell-checker misses many common word errors - read your letter aloud or have a friend listen to it.
- Use bullets, bolding and subheads when appropriate.
- Never use more than two different fonts on any letter.

Watch out . . .

- Don't write a letter or send a reply when you're angry or upset - let it wait a day.
- A letter is always more formal than conversation. Watch your familiarity, tone and language.
- People read E-mail as they do letters, so write messages carefully. Never send in haste.
- Make sure you spell the recipient's name properly. It's worth a phone call to check before you irritate the person to whom you're writing.
- Display fonts and cutesie paper have no place in business communication.